ín and around
alnwick
morpeth
rothbury
warkworth

in and around

alnwick
morpeth
rothbury
warkworth

Ian Smith

sandhill press

My thanks to all who have brightened my days with companionship or conversation, and to those who have enlightened me by their knowledge and help.

to P

The 'Walk' maps are based on Ordnance Survey maps: at about 1:22000 based on Pathfinder 488 (1989); Pathfinder 501 (1989) and Pathfinder 523 (1980); at about 1:45000 based on Landranger 81 (1981), with the permission of the Controller of Her Majesty's Stationery Office. © Crown Copyright.

First published in Great Britain by Sandhill Press Limited, 17 Castle Street, Warkworth, MORPETH, Northumberland, NE65 OUW, 1991
(Warkworth section originally published separately 1990)

Printed by Martins of Berwick, bound by Hunter & Foulis in Great Britain.

Contents

Narrowgate, Alnwick.

River Coquet above Warkworth.

INTRODUCTION

Northumberland has cause to be proud of its country towns. The four in this volume, Alnwick, Morpeth, Rothbury and Warkworth, are lovely places. Each has retained its mediæval layout through centuries of rebuilding, with the old stone passed on from generation to generation of buildings. Each has avoided the worst excesses of modern commercialism. They are fascinating places to explore, with a wealth of history popping up around every corner, with spots of beauty and intriguing eccentricities.

Market Cross and Castle Street, Warkworth

Past each town glides its river, at times placid and peaceful, at others swollen and urgent. The Aln, the Wansbeck and the Coquet add their own beautiful dimension to the towns, which have riverside walks to make the most of them.

This book proffers an exploratory journey on foot around each town, with notes and illustrations of some of the fascinating things you may see. These town visits should be within the capability of most able-bodied people, but steps, stiles and steep sections may be a hazard for those less agile.

Bakehouse Steps, Morpeth

Beyond the towns there are also suggestions for walks in the countryside, either circular or linear (with public transport suggestions for the return). These walks all take some account of the rivers. In some cases they trace the followable sections of river all the way to the sea. In others, where the riverside paths are limited (or dull!), they explore the hillsides, offering views of the river valleys. The longer walks can be split into convenient sections by those who wish to take their time and potter.

The Black Bull, Morpeth

There is plenty to stop for. A perusal of the guide will reveal another theme, apart from towns and rivers. There are castles here. Whether they are the magnificent fortified seats of power, like Alnwick Castle, or the humble ruined peel of Great Tosson, they remind us that this is Border country, frequently fought over in the past, where people found a need for strong defences. There are also dissolved religious houses tucked away in the river valleys, plus a Hermitage. Two towns have chantries near the main bridge, originally for prayer for travellers, but forming a starting point for local education.

Some of these places may be visited (some for a fee), but others retain their privacy.

River crossings abound, from old stepping stones to beautiful stone bridges, from little foot-bridges to tall viaducts.

In between are the trees and woods, hedgerows and pastures, with all their wildlife. Whilst preparing these guides I have seen a red squirrel, a stoat, weasels and rabbits galore. There are herons, ducks and swans on each river, -and much more!

The Market Cross and Armstrong Memorial, Rothbury.

USING THE GUIDE

The book is divided into separate chapters for each of the areas:

    Alnwick,   Morpeth,   Rothbury,   Warkworth.

Each chapter is arranged in the same way:
- an introduction
- a town plan (NOT to scale)
- the contents page
- a guided walking route around the town and its sights.
- other walks starting from the town.
- an index

The out-of-town walks each have a map, with the distance walked marked in kilometres, and an illustrated guide to the walk.

Maps are at a scale of about 1:45000, or 1:22000.

> Walking directions are enclosed in a box and prefaced **✻**
> Alternative routes are denoted by **✻**

Notes about things to be seen begin with ●

Warkworth   iv

An APOLOGY

I owe an apology to inhabitants of Lesbury and Alnmouth, Mitford, Bothal and Newbiggin, and Amble, for collecting them under the banners of Alnwick, Morpeth or Warkworth. I do recognize their independence, but had to organise the chapter headings in some sensible way!

v   Warkworth, Carrickfergus Tower

RIGHTS OF WAY AND PRIVATE PROPERTY

The routes shown on the sketch maps are not evidence of a public right of way, nor are the route descriptions. Most of the footpaths are rights of way (check with Ordnance Survey maps) but there are some sections which are not.

Some belong to the Forestry Commission, who allow reasonable - and free - public access.

One section east of Dove Crag on the Simonsides belongs to the Duke of Northumberland.

All of Hulne Park is private, including the drives and footpaths. It may only be visited at specified times, entering through Forest Lodge:

The Cragside Estate is in the care of the National Trust, and its paths and drives are private. Members may visit free during opening hours, and non-members upon payment of a fee at the Debdon Gate.

The Castle at Alnwick is a private residence, but may be visited, for a fee, during the day in summer.

Warkworth Castle and Hermitage are cared for by English Heritage, who make an admission charge. The castle is opened throughout the year. The Hermitage may only be reached by ferry, during its opening times. (enquire at the Castle). Brinkburn Priory is also English Heritage.

Newminster Abbey is privately owned, but may be visited (by the approved route) during daylight hours.

Morpeth Chantry is a tourist information office and crafts centre, open during working hours.

Other castles, houses and peels are private property, and should be respected as such.

If you visit any of the churches, please remember that they are not just beautiful parts of our cultural history, but places of community worship and prayer. They do not receive state funds for their upkeep, so a donation would be welcome.

Rights of Way ARE shown on Ordnance Survey maps. All the routes in this guide are shown on OS 1:50000 Landranger Sheet 81, "Alnwick, Morpeth and surrounding area"

Please remember that this countryside is a working area.

Crops (including grass) and animals need to be respected by passers-by, and not trampled or scared. Please close gates behind you and take your litter home. Keep dogs under control and away from livestock. Keep yourself — and children — away from farm machinery.

<u>Cragside Home Farm</u> — now the Visitors' Centre.

This area of Northumberland has a useful network of bus services, plus a sparse service of local trains. With a little planning they can be used instead of, or to supplement, private transport, so that you do not always have to walk round in circles!

Northumberland County Council publish public transport guides.

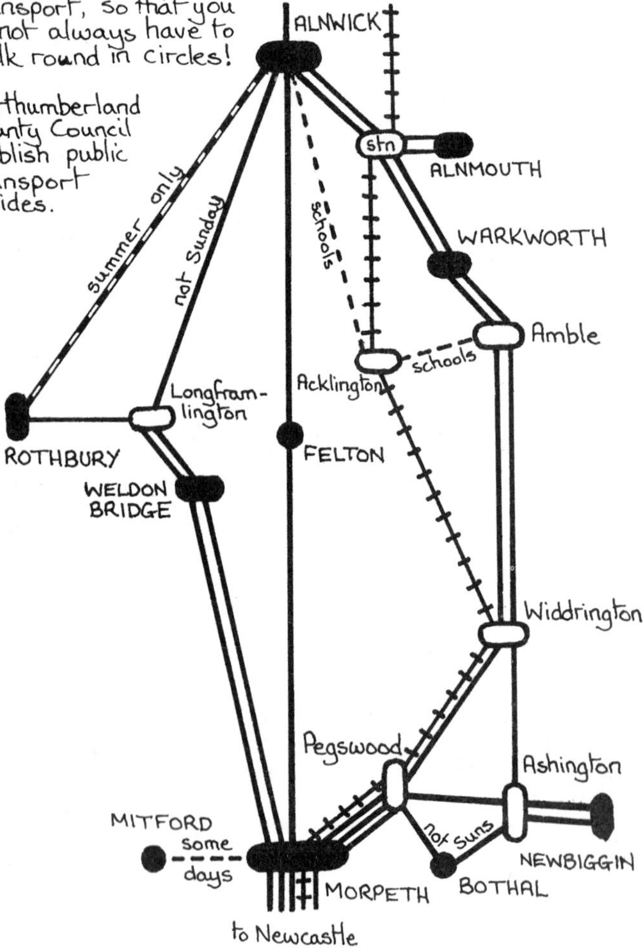

ALNWICK

stn

ALNMOUTH

WARKWORTH

Amble

summer only

not Sunday

schools

Acklington

schools

Longfram-lington

FELTON

ROTHBURY

WELDON BRIDGE

Widdrington

Pegswood

Ashington

MITFORD
some days

not suns

NEWBIGGIN

MORPETH   BOTHAL

to Newcastle

NOTES on MAPS and SYMBOLS.

The maps of the towns are not to scale. Nor do they purport to show everything! They try to show the whereabouts of places mentioned in the guide, plus a few pubs, cafés, sweetie-shops, loos ..... etc. These may change with time of course, or with the seasons. They come and go and change their name. Even bus stations can disappear (as at Rothbury) or move (as at Morpeth)!

The town maps also indicate the route suggested in the guide. But please do not feel constrained to follow my footsteps. The idea is for you to enjoy it. I certainly pottered backwards and forwards, and sat in pubs and cafés in between the energetic bits.

The countryside maps are to two scales: about 1:45000 or about 1:22 000. A scale in kilometres is marked on each one.

They are all the right way up. ie north at the top.

Symbols:

- ▬ ▬ ▬ ▬ } suggested route

- ▬ g/▬ ▬/s ½ f.b , gate, stile, footbridge

- .... 50 ...... contour (50 metre intervals) where helpful.

- ▬ ⑰ ▬ ▬ distance from start in km.

- ♣ ♧ ♣ ♧ ♣ ♧ guess!

Hulne Priory from the Iron Bridge.

ix

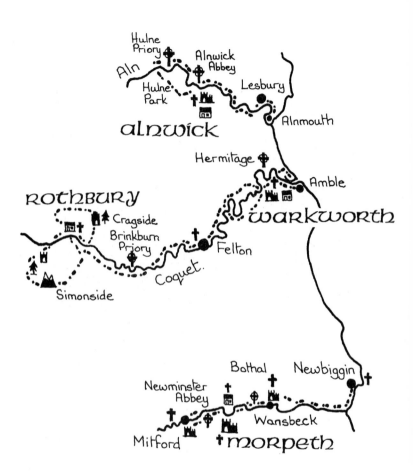

alnwick

Castle Barbican

Alnwick is inextricably entwined with the lords of Northumberland: the Earls of mediaeval times built the Castle to control the Great North Road where it crosses the Aln, and the town grew up in its shelter. The Dukes of the last two centuries or so have made Alnwick their seat, making the castle a stately home and mildly competing with the townspeople to produce a town that has few equals in the country. Cut off from the railway, Alnwick has avoided becoming a dormitory for Newcastle, and is still very much a Northumbrian country town.

Alnwick 2

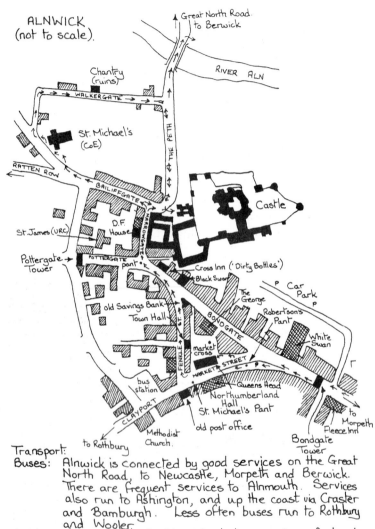

ALNWICK
(not to scale).

Great North Road.
to Berwick

RIVER ALN

Chantry
(ruins)

WALKERGATE

THE PETH

St. Michael's
(CoE)

RATTEN ROW

BAILIFFGATE

Castle

NARROWGATE

D.F.
House

St. James (URC)

Pottergate
Tower

POTTERGATE
pant

Cross Inn ('Dirty Bottles')

Black Swan

old Savings Bank

Town Hall

The George

P Car
Park
P
P

Robertson's
Pant

White
Swan

FENKLE ST.

BONDGATE

market
cross

MARKET STREET

bus
station

Queens Head

Northumberland
Hall

CLAYPORT

St. Michael's Pant

old post office

to
Morpeth
Fleece Inn

Bondgate
Tower

to Rothbury

Methodist
Church.

Transport:

Buses: Alnwick is connected by good services on the Great
North Road, to Newcastle, Morpeth and Berwick.
There are frequent services to Alnmouth. Services
also run to Ashington, and up the coast via Craster
and Bamburgh. Less often buses run to Rothbury
and Wooler.

Trains no longer reach Alnwick, but a number of local
trains serve Alnmouth from Newcastle & Berwick.

The Aln above Canongate Bridge.

Alnwick 4 : Bondgate

* From the massive carparks between Bondgate and the castle park walls — or the bus station — make your way to the Bondgate Tower, a proper place to enter Alnwick. Pass through the Tower and along Bondgate Within, and bear left into Market Street.

● <u>The Bondgate or Hotspur Tower</u> was built as part of the town walls authorised by Henry Ⅵ in 1433. The town, outside the protection of the castle walls, had suffered from the almost regular raids from Scotland. It found it difficult to raise the funds for walls for its own protection. The Earls were pre-occupied with maintaining their own walls and fighting their own battles for power within the land, and had little thought for the town's problems.

Even so the mythology has linked this surviving tower to the most romantic of the Percys — Harry Hotspur — even though he had been killed in battle before it was built!

Other towers, at Clayport, Pottergate and Narrowgate, with linking walls, once defined the mediæval town, but all the others have been demolished as relationships with Scotland improved.

- Market Street sweeps elegantly round towards the market square, with a line of trees separating the sloping cobbles from the main thoroughfare. It is seldom as empty as on Boxing Day (above), but is the commercial hub of the town.

Alnwick has a number of inns, banks, cafés, restaurants, tea-rooms, and shops of all kinds to cater for residents and visitors, mainly in Bondgate and Market Street.

Market day is Saturday

Early closing day is Wednesday.

- Robertson's Pant, a Victorian extravaganza, stands at the junction of Market Street with Bondgate. It was presented by Adam Robertson, a freeman of the town, in 1890.
The tiny polished door to the works is by far the best pant door in Alnwick!

> * Walk up Market Street to
> St Michael's Pant, then cross
> over to Northumberland Hall
> and the Market Place.

• Every market requires at least one
watering place for the animals, and
this is no exception. At the foot
of Market Street we saw Robertson's
Pant. Here, in a very different style,
with an ornate Gothic column but
very functional trough, is St Michael's
Pant. On top are St Michael and the
dragon. It was built in the town's
romantic bloom, in 1765.
Other pants in Alnwick, at Pottergate
and Canongate also show the St Michael
and dragon motif.

• The market in Alnwick dates back to the 13th century,
at least, with an official authority from 1464. Over
the years it has had a series of Market Crosses.
These were mainly in the form of open buildings for the
sale of butter and eggs. These were replaced by a
larger shambles building,
with an open arcade facing
north onto the square, which
in turn was replaced by
the Northumberland Hall.
The cross in the market
place is the Town Cross,
the place for proclamations.
Alnwick has revived its
practice of holding a Fair
for a week from the last
Sunday in May Alnwick
sees mediaeval costume,
entertainments, crafts,
mummers, a ducking
stool ......, all the
fun of the
mediaeval fair!

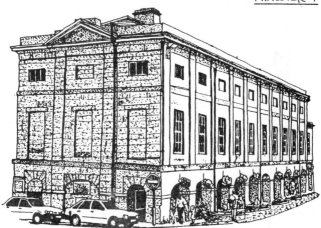

• The Northumberland Hall

In a spirit of friendly rivalry with the towns-people the 3rd Duke had this grand hall built in 1826, outshining the nearby Town Hall.

The 8th Duke made a gift of it to the Alnwick Urban District Council in 1919.

It was restored in 1981, and now houses the tourist information office as well as several shops under the arches.

(There are public toilets on the Market Place side).

Upstairs is an assembly room.

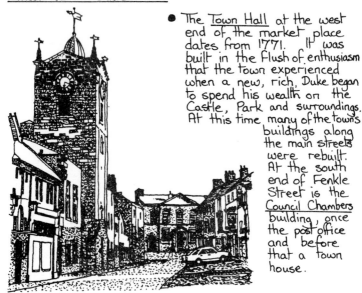

- The <u>Town Hall</u> at the west end of the market place dates from 1771. It was built in the flush of enthusiasm that the town experienced when a new, rich, Duke began to spend his wealth on the Castle, Park and surroundings. At this time many of the town's buildings along the main streets were rebuilt. At the south end of Fenkle Street is the <u>Council Chambers</u> building, once the post office and before that a town house.

* From the Market Place go through the archway, through the Town Hall, into Fenkle Street. Turn north and descend into Narrowgate.

- Fenkle Street meets Bondgate at a sharp angle, which is neatly filled by the <u>Old Savings Bank</u> (1835).

● Narrowgate creeps round the castle walls. It contains a couple of the old inns — the Black Swan (right) and the Old Cross (below). Here the stage coaches for North-umberland would stop before heading for the moors.

● The Old Cross (named after the de Vescy cross on the wall) has become famous for its Dirty Bottles. The story is that the innkeeper died while dressing the window, about 150 years ago. His widow refused to let the bottles be disturbed. Legend holds that any disturbance would be fatal, so the bottles remain in the window, attracting dust and customers.

● The pant at the foot of Pottergate dates from 1873, and stands on the site of an older pant.

The Bow Burn flows under here, to pass under Bow Alley and round the castle walls. Once it formed the castle's southern moat, and itself was a point for cattle to refresh them-selves.

Alnwick 10 : Narrowgate

- If you look west up Pottergate you cannot miss the sight of Pottergate Tower on the skyline.

This Gothic Tower replaced the mediœval tower in 1765, at the expense of the Duke.
The side facing the town — and castle — is much more ornate than that facing west!
It used to sport a delicate lanthorn like that on St. Nicholas' Cathedral in Newcastle, but in 1812 it suffered storm damage and was removed, despite public protest.

---

* Continue along Narrowgate beside the castle walls to Bailliffgate.

Narrowgate

• Partway along
Narrowgate is the Red House,
otherwise known as Dorothy Forster Court.
This is immediately recognisable, being a stone
house faced in red brick! If you tried to get
planning permission for this in Alnwick today, you
would almost certainly be refused as out of character!
Dorothy Forster became one of Northumberland's heroines
following the abortive rising of 1715. Her brother Tom,
general in the rebellion, was imprisoned in Newgate,
in London. Dorothy made her way to the capital, where
she acquired skeleton keys. By bribery and misdirection
she contrived her brother's escape to France, before
she returned to Northumberland.

> ✻ Turn left along Bailliffgate to the Parish Church.

● <u>Bailliffgate</u> was outside the mediaeval town walls, and was probably called Baileygate (from its position). Here the troops from the castle would exercise. Now it boasts a number of buildings in the mellow local sandstone. The regularly pollarded trees look almost artificial in summer with their dense spheres of foliage

● <u>St. Michael's</u> is unusual in Northumberland for its Perpendicular style. The 15th century was not a rich period for the county, and few churches were built. But the old Norman church (of which traces are visible in the rebuild) was badly in need of repair. A thorough and beautiful job was done.

- The south-east corner of St. Michael's has a small extra tower: a staircase leads up to a small cell. This was a dwelling for a chantry priest, but would have doubled as a lookout, part of the town's early warning system.

- If St Michael's is open go in. The church offers a really good leaflet describing the internal features of interest.

* Go down the steps outside the main tower. Turn east along Walkergate. At the end turn down to the Lion Bridge (p.20), or up to the Castle.

- The Chantry. Founded in 1449 the chantry chapel developed into a free school, the first Alnwick Grammar School. Now little is left — just walled-up windows and a doorway in the wall.

Alnwick 14 : The Castle

The Aln is the first river crossing on the Great North Road south of the old border — the Tweed. The road itself picks a way along the eastern slopes of the high ground on its way from Berwick, and naturally comes to the Aln at this point. So there had to be a castle here. As the Norman barons settled into England after 1066 Northumberland became a buffer state between Scotland and England. In 1093 a Scottish king, Malcolm, was killed just a mile north of here.

The basic motte and bailey layout of the castle dates back to Yvo de Vescy, who became owner of Alnwick in 1096. Some of the bailey walls date back to this time. Twelfth century masonry can be identified by its small stones, laid parallel to the ground rather than horizontally. The de Vescy family held the castle for two hundred years of turbulent history, besieged at times by the Scots or by English kings. At times they were on the outside, trying to get in!

Their tenure was followed by that of the Percy family, with whom the castle has been associated ever since. The Lords Percy of Alnwick rebuilt and strengthened the castle, adding many towers in the 14th century, some of which survive.

The Percys became Earls of Northumberland as well as Lords of Alnwick. They held the castle as a secure base through another three hundred years of warfare. Not only were there wars with the Scots, and Border raiding, but the English wars of Succession too, as the throne passed from family to family. The Percys played a significant, if not always successful, part, as one of the most powerful families in the land.

After the Union with Scotland in 1606 the Northern March became less important politically, and the Earls moved south. Alnwick Castle became a ruin.

Its fortunes revived when Sir Hugh Smithson, who had married the heiress to the Barony of Alnwick, took the name of Percy and succeeded to the title of Earl. Later, in 1766 he was created Duke of Northumberland. He began the task of rebuilding the castle as a home, together with the local estates, which has been carried on by the family ever since.

Alnwick 16 : Castle Baileys

Alnwick Castle is private property, the home of the Percy family, Dukes of Northumberland. Visitors are welcomed at certain times, to visit the baileys, the coach-house and family apartments.

The Castle has its own guide-book which gives comprehensive detail about the castle, its history and the family.

Visitors approach past the <u>Barbican</u> (p3), a fortress in its own right, with three doors, a moat and drawbridge to pass. The stone figures are 19th century. You go through into the coachyard, and enter the outer bailey past the <u>Clock Tower</u>

Falconer's Tower ↓ (C19)

Abbot's Tower → (1310)

Terrace

Constable's Tower (1310)

Barbican (1440) →

public entrance →

Prudhoe Tower (1854)

Gatehouse ← (1440)

Chapel (1854)

Postern Tower (1310)

well

Middle Bailey

Outer Bailey

Record Tower (1885)

Clock Tower

Middle Gate →

Octagonal Towers (1350)

Eastern Garret

← shop

Warder's Tower (1854)

Auditor's Tower

- The <u>Prudhoe Tower and Chapel</u> were built onto the keep in 1854. Much of the rest of the keep is 1764 building by the 1st Duke, on the site of the mediæval keep, using much of its material. The keep used to form the north wall of the castle here, until the <u>Terrace</u> was added in 1865.

- <u>Cannon</u> are a symbol of the mediæval castle's decline: one salvo from a siege train and this type of castle surrendered!

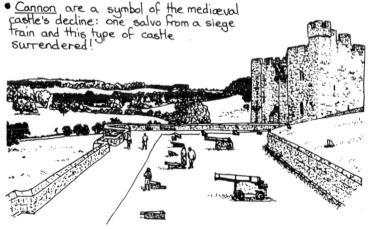

- You enter the Inner Ward — the courtyard within the Keep — through a <u>Norman Archway</u>. This forms the inner half of the passage — you can see the join — as the Keep walls were thickened in the 14th century. The arch bears the characteristic Norman tooling.

- The <u>well</u> and its mechanism date in part to the 14th century, with the 'saint' above added in the 18th century.

- In the Ward you will see the copy of the <u>lamp</u> on the Palazzo Vecchio in Florence. This reflects the 4th Duke's combination of mediæval fortress with Italian Renaissance art.

- The Entrance Hall of the castle contains the armoury of the Percy Tenantry Volunteers, a force raised during the Napoleonic wars. It reminds us that the Percys once had the largest 'private' army in England, back in mediæval times.

• Although several of the towers around the bailey walls have been maintained in almost original condition, the Keep has been rebuilt twice since 1765, when the first Duke engaged Robert Adam to produce a Gothic mansion. The 4th Duke did not share his tastes, preferring a contrast between austere mediæval exteriors and Renaissance opulence inside. He had the Prudhoe Tower added as a tall tower to draw the eye, and had the interior refurnished in an Italian style. If you have not looked in the Castle guidebook the richness of the interior may take your breath away. It is magnificent! Perhaps best of all is the staircase, with each step formed from a single 4 metre wide slab of polished Rothbury stone, sweeping up to the light and airy Guard Room.

For all its grandeur and its treasures, it manages to remain a home rather than a museum. It is worth a visit!

The Norman
Gateway

✳ The easy way back to Bondgate is to turn left along Narrowgate, and back through the town. But the stroll through the Pastures offers fresh air and great views. So.....

From the Castle entrance go down to the Lion Bridge over the Aln. Just beyond, a gate opens onto the Pastures. Admire these best views of the castle as you follow the path downstream to Denwick Bridge. From there follow the winding road uphill beside the Park wall to reach the War Memorial and Tenantry Column. Turn right along the road to reach Bondgate.

● The Lion Bridge dates from 1773.

● The Pastures are the scene of the Shrove Tuesday football match, played between the youths of the parishes of St Mark & St Paul.

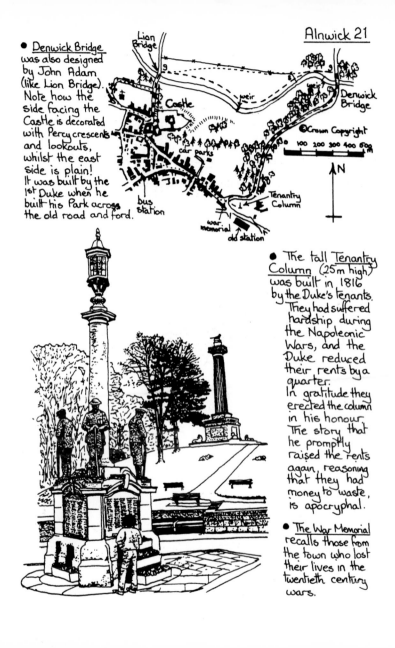

• <u>Denwick Bridge</u> was also designed by John Adam (like Lion Bridge). Note how the side facing the Castle is decorated with Percy crescents and lookouts, whilst the east side is plain! It was built by the 1st Duke when he built his Park across the old road and ford.

Lion Bridge

Castle

weir

Denwick Bridge

©Crown Copyright

100 200 300 400 500

N

car parks

bus station

Tenantry Column

war memorial

old station

• The tall <u>Tenantry Column</u> (25m high) was built in 1816 by the Duke's tenants. They had suffered hardship during the Napoleonic Wars, and the Duke reduced their rents by a quarter.
In gratitude they erected the column in his honour. The story that he promptly raised the rents again, reasoning that they had money to waste, is apocryphal.

• The War Memorial recalls those from the town who lost their lives in the twentieth century wars.

Forest Lodge

HULNE PARK

PUBLIC ACCESS TO HULNE PARK
IS PERMITTED ON FOOT ONLY ON
SATURDAYS AND SUNDAYS BETWEEN
1PM AND SUNSET. SPECIAL PASSES
FOR OTHER DAYS MAY BE AVAILABLE
FROM THE ESTATES OFFICE ALNWICK
CASTLE WHERE ALL ENQUIRIES
SHOULD BE MADE

NO CARS. BICYCLES OR DOGS ARE ADMITTED

Most of this walk is in Hulne Park, which is private property with no rights of way. So access is by permission only. Normally this is freely given on Saturdays and Sundays between 1pm and sunset. The notice on the left is on the gate at Forest Lodge, which is the only public entrance. (You may leave by the Lodges at Alnwick Abbey and Friars Well, but not enter there).

* From the Castle go west along Bailliffgate, and keep straight on up Ratten Row (where the cavalry used to be exercised) towards Forest Lodge. Just before the lodge you can see the stone commemorating the capture of William the Lion, King of Scotland, in 1172. If the Park is open, follow the drive along to cross the Stocking Burn, then continue past Moor Lodge along Farm Drive, enjoying the views. A wooden hut stands by the junction with Tower Drive. Go left, up the hill and bear left on a track under the trees near the top. This takes you on a circuit to Nine Year Old Hole and Brizlee Tower.
(continued...)

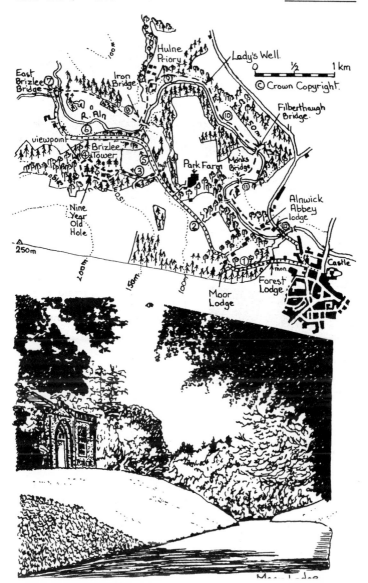

Hulne Priory

Lady's Well.

0　　½　　1 km
© Crown Copyright.

East Brizlee Bridge ⑦

Iron Bridge

Filberthaugh Bridge.

R. Aln

⑧

⑥

viewpoint

Brizlee Tower

④

③

⑤

100m

⑩

50m

Park Farm

Monks Bridge

⑪

Nine Year Old Hole

150m

②

Alnwick Abbey Lodge

⑨

△ 250m

200m

150m

100m

①

Moor Lodge

Forest Lodge

mon.

mon.

Castle

Alnwick 24 : Brizlee Hill.

If you go clockwise round the circuit on top of Brizlee Hill you will, on the south side, see a solitary figure standing ahead. As you come closer you will discover the <u>stone hermit</u>. He probably dates from the 1st Duke's romantic development of the Park's features, in 1765.
He guards the <u>Nine Year Aad Hole</u> — probably once the chosen abode of an old horse.

A legend associated with the cave is a tale of three thieves falling out: having hidden a treasure chest here, one went to town to fetch bread. Another murdered him on his way back, to be stabbed in the back by the third. He ate the bread, which had been poisoned by the first, so no-one knows where the treasure is hidden!

A stone and seat mark the <u>viewpoint</u>. Sit and enjoy the countryside laid out below you, and the prospect of the Cheviot Hills, not far away. Around you the hill may buzz with wild-life. A red squirrel, rabbits, wrens, jays and magpies were seen in one ten-minute sojourn here.

● Brizlee Tower stands on the summit of the hill. 24 metres high, it was erected by the 1st Duke in 1781. He favoured this Gothic style. It is an excellent lookout point, and sports a brazier on top. From the balcony it is possible to see seven castles: Alnwick, Warkworth, Holy Island, Ros, Chillingham, Dunstanburgh and Bamburgh. The tower is not open for visitors.

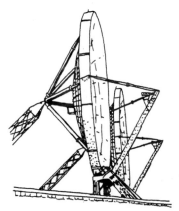

Brizlee Tower with its brazier formed part of the Napoleonic War Early Warning System. Any invasion in the north could be signalled round the country by a chain of beacons. Further up on the moors, but visible from Brizlee Hill, is the modern equivalent, with the Royal Signals relay station, transmitting and receiving information around the country. (You may not visit them!)

* From Brizlee Tower return
down Tower Drive, eastwards.
As you descend you should be
able to see Hulne Priory down
beyond the river, on your left.
Turn left when you reach
Park Drive, and follow it
north round the flank of
Brizlee Hill. When you emerge
from the woods the drive curves
round to the north, passing
East Brizlee.
You cross the Aln by East
Brizlee Bridge, and turn east
along Palmstrother Drive. This
takes you across the Aln's
flood-plain, which sports
several ox-bow lakes, showing
where the river used to flow.
At the Iron Bridge turn left,
and beyond the gate climb
the hill to Hulne Priory.

• Hulne Priory is still
inhabited by Friars,
but only in stone.
They were carved by
a local craftsman,
Matthew Mills
in 1777.

• Hulne Priory was a Carmelite foundation from about 1240 AD, during the de Vescy tenure of Alnwick. Apparently, Brizlee Hill reminded its founder, Ralph Fresborn - a knight turned friar - of Mount Carmel.

Its distance from Alnwick Castle (two miles or so) made self-defence rather important, so the priory was enclosed in a massive wall. This survives, even if it has lost its corner towers and parapet. A peel tower was built inside by the 4th Earl in 1488.

Eastern Gateway.

The Dissolution of the Monasteries in 1539 swept away the White Friars, but the buildings were too far from town to be a convenient quarry. As they were also on the Earls' land much has survived.

You can enter by the door on the south-west corner. Inside you will find the pele tower, rebuilt as a hunting lodge by the 1st Duke in pseudo-Gothic style in 1777. The ornate eastern gateway dates from then too. Various of the monastic buildings have been rebuilt for estate functions, but you can still identify the principal church, chapter house and cloister. The priory is still a place of charm, beauty and peace.

Filberthaugh Bridge.

• Hulne Park has long
been the park of the Earls
and Dukes, but it was extended
by the 1st Duke's purchase of Alnwick
Abbey. He had the park re-shaped, with the road to
Eglingham re-routed outside the wall. Capability Brown
landscaped the park to good effect.

Duchess's Bridge

✳ From Hulne Priory follow the path descending eastwards along the riverbank. The Aln here flows through a narrow wooded valley. After about 700 metres you pass Lady's Well (below). Stay on the track until you reach Filberthaugh Bridge. Cross over, and follow the track on downstream to either Monk's Bridge (similar to Filberthaugh Bridge) or Duchess' Bridge, where cross to the east bank. The track continues downriver to Alnwick Abbey, then leaves the estate by the Lodge. Turn right along the road outside the Park, cross the river by Canongate Bridge, and climb up Canongate. You pass through an estate of Percy houses, dedicated to the memory of several Dukes and Duchesses. Note the pant, just before you meet Rotten Row. Canongate joins Bailliffgate, which you follow back towards the Castle.

Lady's Well.

● Alnwick Abbey

A Premonstratensian abbey of White Canons was founded here in 1147 — the second in England. It enjoyed the protection of the nearby castle. It remained until the Dissolution in 1539. Only the gatehouse and under-ground foundations remain.

<u>Looking back to Alnwick Castle from Denwick Bridge.</u>

<u>The first set of stepping stones.</u>

@ Alnwick to Old Hawkhill Stepping Stones.

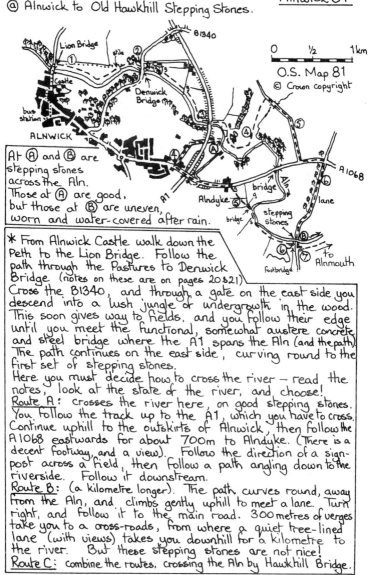

O.S. Map 81
© Crown copyright

At Ⓐ and Ⓑ are stepping stones across the Aln. Those at Ⓐ are good, but those at Ⓑ are uneven, worn and water-covered after rain.

✻ From Alnwick Castle walk down the Peth to the Lion Bridge. Follow the path through the Pastures to Denwick Bridge (notes on these are on pages 20 & 21).
Cross the B1340, and through a gate on the east side you descend into a lush jungle of undergrowth in the wood. This soon gives way to fields, and you follow their edge until you meet the functional, somewhat austere concrete and steel bridge where the A1 spans the Aln (and the path). The path continues on the east side, curving round to the first set of stepping stones.
Here you must decide how to cross the river — read the notes, look at the state of the river, and choose!
Route A: crosses the river here, on good stepping stones. You follow the track up to the A1, which you have to cross. Continue uphill to the outskirts of Alnwick, then follow the A1068 eastwards for about 700m to Alndyke. (There is a decent footway, and a view). Follow the direction of a sign-post across a field, then follow a path angling down to the riverside. Follow it downstream.
Route B: (a kilometre longer). The path curves round, away from the Aln, and climbs gently uphill to meet a lane. Turn right, and follow it to the main road. 300 metres of verges take you to a cross-roads, from where a quiet tree-lined lane (with views) takes you downhill for a kilometre to the river. But these stepping stones are not nice!
Route C: combine the routes, crossing the Aln by Hawkhill Bridge.

The <u>viaduct</u> was built as part of the Newcastle to Berwick railway in about 1846, and remained essentially the same until 1990 when the electrification masts were added. It is still a good place to view trains hurtling to and from Scotland.

<u>Lesbury</u> is a charming suburban village. It has a post office stores to refresh the weary. The church dates in part from the 13th century. Look for the crescent marks of the Percys on houses, and in the church.

ⓑ Old Hawkhill Stepping Stones to Alnmouth

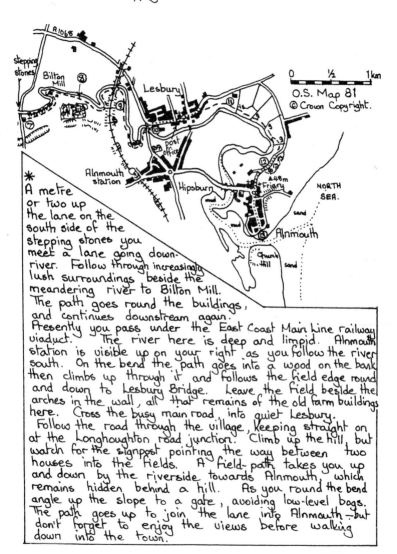

0   ½   1 km

O.S. Map 81
© Crown Copyright.

* A metre
or two up
the lane on the
south side of the
stepping stones you
meet a lane going down-
river. Follow through increasingly
lush surroundings beside the
meandering river to Bilton Mill.
The path goes round the buildings,
and continues downstream again.
Presently you pass under the East Coast Main Line railway
viaduct.   The river here is deep and limpid. Alnmouth
station is visible up on your right as you follow the river
south. On the bend the path goes into a wood on the bank
then climbs up through it and follows the field edge round
and down to Lesbury Bridge. Leave the field beside the
arches in the wall, all that remains of the old farm buildings
here. Cross the busy main road, into quiet Lesbury.
Follow the road through the village, keeping straight on
at the Longhoughton road junction. Climb up the hill, but
watch for the signpost pointing the way between two
houses into the fields. A field-path takes you up
and down by the riverside towards Alnmouth, which
remains hidden behind a hill. As you round the bend
angle up the slope to a gate, avoiding low-level bogs.
The path goes up to join the lane into Alnmouth — but
don't forget to enjoy the views before walking
down into the town.

The Aln meanders back westwards just above Alnmouth.

Northumberland Street, Alnmouth.

● Alnmouth, with its tight-knit cluster of red roofs, is a familiar sight for travellers on the railway or the A1068 road, who see it across the final meanders of the Aln. It retains its charm on closer inspection: the old grain port for the corn-lands of Northumberland has made the transition to residential town and quiet holiday resort with some elegance.

Nature has played its part in the shaping of modern Alnmouth. In 1806 a great storm carved the present river exit to the North Sea, cutting off Church Hill from the town. This storm also completed the ruination of the old Norman church, St. Waleric's. It took another 70 years before the new church was opened in the town. But as Alnmouth had been castigated as "famous for all kinds of wickedness" by John Wesley perhaps this is not surprising! Nowadays the town's reputation is somewhat different — it even has a Franciscan Friary at the north end of town.

Alnmouth has cafés, restaurants, shops, inns, bed and breakfast accommodation and hotels to cater for the tired walker. You may want to walk down to the actual mouth of the Aln, or cool your feet on the beautiful beach of fine sand.

North and south stretch the marvelous beaches of the Northumberland Coastline — but that's another walk or two, and another book!

Frequent buses operate to Alnwick, to return you to your starting point.

Church Hill

Alnwick Index

morpeth

Morpeth is a triumph of everyday economics over the dictates of good defence. The castle is in the classic position, high on the hill on the English side, and well clear of floods. The town, though, is on the good flat land next to the river, a good market place to receive the two roads from Scotland — the High Road via Wooler and the moors, and the Low Road via Alnwick and Berwick. The town paid for it at times — the Scots seemed to treat it as a free market now and then in the Middle Ages. But it survived and flourished. Now it is the County town (although County Hall also lurks up the southern hill, even beyond the church!) and town and river sit beautifully together amid the trees.

Morpeth 2:

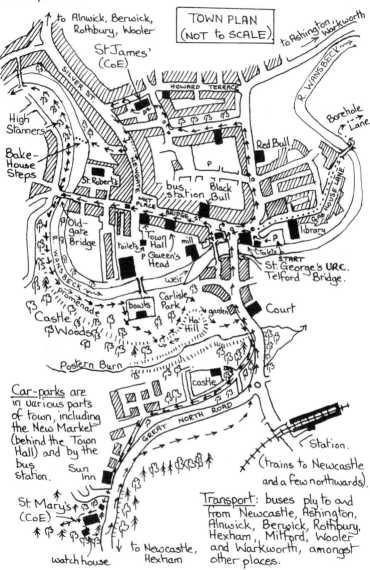

TOWN PLAN (NOT to SCALE)

to Alnwick, Berwick, Rothbury, Wooler

to Ashington, Warkworth

R. WANSBECK

St James' (CoE)

SILVER ST.

HOWARD TERRACE

Borehole Lane

High Stanners

Red Bull

NEWGATE

HOUSE LANE

Bake-House Steps

St. Robert's

bus station

Black Bull

GAS

library

MKT PLACE

BRIDGE ST.

Old-gate Bridge

toilets

Town Hall

mill

P

toilets

R. WANSBECK

P Queen's Head

START
St. George's URC.
Telford Bridge.

weir

Carlisle Park

garden

Court

promenade

bowls

Ha' Hill

Castle Woods

Postern Burn

Castle

Car-parks are in various parts of town, including the New Market (behind the Town Hall) and by the bus station.

GREAT NORTH ROAD

Station.
(trains to Newcastle and a few northwards).

Sun Inn

St. Mary's (CoE)

to Newcastle, Hexham

watch house

Transport: buses ply to and from Newcastle, Ashington, Alnwick, Berwick, Rothbury, Hexham, Mitford, Wooler and Warkworth, amongst other places.

Morpeth 4: The Chantry

Morpeth's main street is Bridge Street, running from the market place to the bridge over the Wansbeck.

In the best tradition the bridge has its own chapel. This began as a 13th century chantry – a chapel where continuous prayers were sung for benefactors and travellers, and where tolls for the bridge were collected! Some of its walls can still be seen on the north side, facing the street. The walled-up arch of the erstwhile north transept can be seen, together with the priest's door.

The chantry was abolished in 1547, along with all others, by Henry VIII. The chantry school was abolished too, but was reinstated by Edward VI's royal charter in 1552. Morpeth Grammar School remained in part of the building for another three hundred years, until it moved to new premises in 1859.

Growth of population in the town increased the problem of having the parish church so far away up the hill. So in 1738 a chapel of ease was built on the south side of the chantry. This use too came to an end when St. James' was opened in the town in 1846.

The chantry building became a mineral-water manufactory, with shops on the street frontage. Now it has been cleaned and tidied up, housing the Tourist Information Office, a Bagpipe Museum and an excellent Crafts Centre.

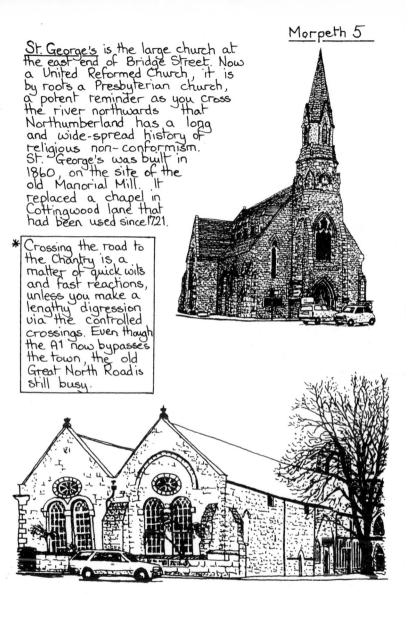

St. George's is the large church at the east end of Bridge Street. Now a United Reformed Church, it is by roots a Presbyterian church, a potent reminder as you cross the river northwards that Northumberland has a long and wide-spread history of religious non-conformism. St. George's was built in 1860, on the site of the old Manorial Mill. It replaced a chapel in Cottingwood lane that had been used since 1721.

* Crossing the road to the Chantry is a matter of quick wits and fast reactions, unless you make a lengthy digression via the controlled crossings. Even though the A1 now bypasses the town, the old Great North Road is still busy.

* Continue west along Bridge St. to the market place. Go past the clocktower and down Oldgate to the river.

• There are several inns of interest along Bridge Street : the Black Bull has a three-storey Regency bow front, and the Queen's Head Hotel has a mock-Tudor style and false gables (added in the 1930's).

• The town hall faces onto the market place, (which is just a road junction nowadays). It was built in 1714 by Vanbrugh, but suffered severe fire damage. In 1870 it was rebuilt in a slightly less heavy style (yes!) at the expense of the lord of the manor – the Earl of Carlisle. (The plain west side originally abutted another building).

• <u>The clock tower</u> in Oldgate looks older than it is. It was built in 1604 using mediæval stone. Later, in 1705 it was heightened to house a peal of six bells. These were given by General Main, governor of Berwick, who was M.P. for Morpeth. As Berwick had had a church built during the Commonwealth in 1652 without a bell-tower, this gave rise to the saying that:

"Berwick bells are heard in Morpeth". Isolated clock-towers like this are rare. Its existence is probably due to the parish church being so far out of town.

The clock came from Bothal Castle. Note that it has no minute marks — between the hours the quarters are shown, as the clock originally had only one hand, like that at Wallington Hall.

• <u>The Hollon Fountain</u> stands in the market-place. It was built in 1885, and stood where a large market building had been. The butter market moved into the town hall, and a small shelter was erected against the east side of the clocktower for a while.

> * Cross Oldgate Bridge. You may wish to perambulate briefly along the green banks towards the Bakehouse Steps, before turning back downriver to join the promenade towards Carlisle Park.

• <u>Oldgate Bridge</u> was rebuilt in 1974. The previous bridge was a girder bridge for light traffic, with a ford alongside. The bridge before that can still be seen! It was moved in 1932, right through the town to the Low Stanners, where it is still in use.

• <u>The Stanners</u> are the stony patches inside the curves of the river. These, opposite Oldgate, are the High Stanners, and have been grassed over.

• <u>The ducks</u> will probably come to pester you if you stay in one place long enough. They <u>expect</u> to be fed!

The Bakehouse Steps

The Wansbeck sweeps round towards Carlisle Park.
The dark tree-shadowed slopes of Castle Woods are
contrasted neatly by the plantings of light-foliaged
trees on the town bank, which catch the sunshine.

* From Oldgate Bridge follow the Promenade below Castle Woods, round the bend, and slightly up into Carlisle Park.

• Carlisle Park once formed part of the Castle grounds, open grazing land stretching up from the river to the Castle walls. The old footway to Newminster, useful when the river was too high to use the stepping stones, ran along its lower slopes. The Countess Rosalind, wife of the Earl of Carlisle, presented the area to the town in 1916, and the towns--people raised the money to landscape and plant it. The Promenade was built in 1930 to replace the muddy footpath and prevent the continuous erosion of the south bank. The Park is a popular place, much used and loved by the townspeople as well as visitors.

• The Bowling Club in the centre of the Park continues a long Morpeth tradition of bowls. Although it has been on this site only since 1926, the town has had a bowling green since at least 1685, when the green outside the Castle gatehouse was granted for the purpose.

• The Elliott Bridge (left) joins the Park with the town. It was built in 1925, then replaced 60cm higher in 1982. On the north bank here rowing boats can be hired. If you fancy a swim, use the swimming baths here, not the river. It is very deep here, and has claimed several lives.

Ha' Hill

• Ha' (or Hall) Hill was the site of the first castle, a Norman motte and bailey made of timber, overlooking the river crossing. It was replaced by the present castle in the twelfth century.

---

* You can climb up onto Ha' Hill quite easily from Carlisle Park. Go up the hill behind the bowls club, and walk along the ridge to the castle mound. The views – over the town, over the Gaol and across the Postern Burn to the Castle, are worth the effort and show why this site was chosen. Unless you are a roughneck looking for a steep descent return to the Park the same way, then follow footpaths round its foot into gardens opposite the Court House. Join the old A1, briefly, and turn right up the old road that climbs up below the Castle walls.

The Castle seen from Ha' Hill

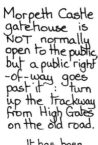

Morpeth Castle gatehouse is NOT normally open to the public, but a public right-of-way goes past it : turn up the trackway from High Gates on the old road.

It has been restored by the Landmark Trust.

● Very little remains of the twelfth century castle built by the de Merlays, who were given permission to "pacify" the manor by William the Conqueror. It was mostly demolished by King John in his rampage against the northern barons. The gatehouse was built in the late fourteenth century, but suffered, along with the curtain walls, in the Civil War, when all the interior buildings were destroyed. By marriage the manor passed along, through the Greystokes and the Dacres, to the Howards, who became Earls of Carlisle. In about 1850 the Earl had the gatehouse rebuilt as a residence, in its present form.

● Not a castle! Morpeth's <u>Court House</u> is the most impressive of the town's military-style buildings. It was built in 1822 as the gatehouse to the County Gaol. Dobson's appreciation of Edward I's Welsh castles is obvious!

HighGrates

• The Great North Road used to climb up from the Bridge, avoiding the bogs of the Church Beck valley, to pass close under the watchful eyes of Morpeth Castle.

As you continue along the narrow lane beyond HighGrates – the crossroads below the Castle gatehouse – it is difficult to believe that this was the main road between the English and Scottish capitals. (But that can still be said of parts of the present A1 in Northumberland!).

NEWCASTLE	14
DARLINGTON	46½
YORK	95
LONDON	289

✻ A little way beyond HighGrates it branches down to the left, just a foot-way wide, to rejoin the newer road near the Sun Inn.

Climb up the hill to the Parish Church of St. Mary.

● Many a parishioner must have been grateful for the seat in the wall below the castle – it was, and is, a long way to walk up to the church from the town. Tradition holds that the seat was also used to rest coffins.

The raised cobbled walkway was ordered in 1690 by the Earl of Carlisle, as the roadway was so awful to walk on.

● The road was diverted down the valley of the Church Burn, and through the end of Castle Hill, in 1828 as part of the approach to the new Telford Bridge. The Church Burn itself was culverted, and its cutting filled in to make the patch of park, just after World War 2.

The old and 'new' roads meet by the Sun Inn, just below St. Mary's.

Morpeth 16 : St. Mary's Church.

● St. Mary's occupies the high ground just where the main road starts to dip down from the flat Northumberland plain into the narrow cutting of the Wansbeck Valley. The church is surrounded by trees and greenery: huge sequoia and wellingtonia, a century old, grace the churchyard to the west, whilst ancient yews darken the approach and immediate surroundings of the church. The churchyard itself is a fascinating place to explore. By the tower lie the remnants of two mediæval tomb effigies.

Your approach to the church takes you past beautifully kept gardens and through the 1861-built lychgate. The church building itself was built mainly in the 14th century, on an earlier site, with Victorian restoration. The east window is perhaps its greatest architectural treasure. Containing the best 14th century glass in the county, it depicts the dream of Jesse.

- The <u>churchyard watch-house</u> stands guard beside the alleyway leading down to the A1. It was built in 1831 at a time when cadavers commanded a good price in the medical school at Newcastle. The high road provided a convenient escape route for the grave-robbers and their booty.

- <u>Emily Davison</u> is buried in the churchyard. Emily was the Suffragete who died after throwing herself under the

hooves of George V's horse on Derby Day in 1913. She had already achieved fame (or notoriety) for her militant acts calling attention to the lack of a universal franchise: she was chained to railings; imprisoned; went on hunger strike; was force-fed; led demonstrations..... to upset the Establishment of the day. Her funeral procession to St. Mary's was attended by thousands of people (men as well as women), who lined the road up from the town.

Morpeth 18: Bridges.

> * Descend the main road again, passing Deuchar Park. From here you obtain a different perspective on the hill-top castle, unappreciated by most passing motorists.

• Up on your right is one of Morpeth's railway stations. It used to have two when the Blyth and Tyne, and North British Railways were in competition with the North Eastern. The very sharp curve on the main line was the scene of an horrific accident in 1969 when the 'Aberdonian' came off the rails at speed, into the gardens up above you.

> * Continue down the hill, past the Gaol to the Toll House and the Telford Bridge.

• The old bridge dates from the 13th century, and should have been demolished completely when the Telford Bridge was built alongside in 1832. Its upkeep was paid for by the Chantry tolls, but it was a narrow, awkward, double-humped bridge, unsuitable for the stage coaches as they grew larger. Indeed, two fell off it! The arches were duly demolished to prevent avoidance of tolls on the new bridge, but the central pier and abutments remained. A wooden footway was installed, but soon decayed. It was replaced by an iron footbridge made locally in 1869.

The elegant Telford Bridge was engineered by Thomas Telford, designed by John Dobson. They had the skill and foresight to produce a bridge capable of handling today's traffic and vehicles — a far cry from the wagons and carriages of 1830.

Swinney's footbridge

- Upstream from the bridges the most prominent building is Oliver's Mill, with its weir. It used to mill corn. It is a reminder that central Morpeth had its industry too: once it was a centre for the tanning industry, with cattle from Scotland and local oak-bark.

- The Toll-house, just south of the Telford Bridge, took tolls for sixteen years, until the new bridge was paid for. Since then it has had a variety of uses. Now it is an off-licence.

Morpeth 20: the Victorian town.

* Turn right at the north end of the Telford Bridge, past St. George's. Cross the road, and follow Damside and Dark Lane, past the Old Red Bull until you reach Dacre Street. Turn up this avenue, which gives an impression of what the Victorian town developers wanted for their town. As well as solid houses we find here a healthy regard for the urban value of trees. No miniatures or flowering cherries here, but real trees — too many planners seem scared of them, but this shows their value. At the end of Dacre Street turn right along Well Way to reach St. James.

• Part of the centuries-old pattern of Morpeth survives in this Victorian development area. The old properties along Bridge Street and Newgate had long burgages, stretching back to the river or - on this side - back alleys. It is these alleys that survive, as Cottingwood Lane, Well Way and Back Riggs, with Copper Chare to link them with Newgate.

• The <u>church of St James the Great</u> is a grand example of Norman architecture – built in 1846! This Victorian era saw a population explosion in the town, which was accommodated by a wave of new building on the old orchards to the north of the town. Terraces were also built on the burgages south of Oldgate. All these people were not going to trudge all the way up the hill to St. Mary's, and the Chantry, despite its extension, was too small and not safe. The Rector of Morpeth, Rev. Francis Grey, had St. James' built.

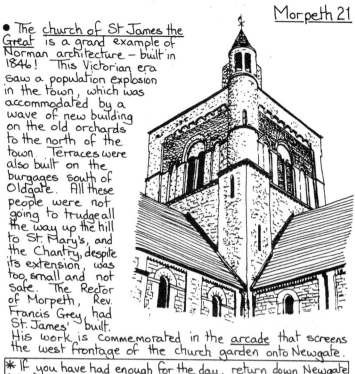

His work is commemorated in the <u>arcade</u> that screens the west frontage of the church garden onto Newgate.

* If you have had enough for the day, return down Newgate into the Market Place, and locate your transportation!

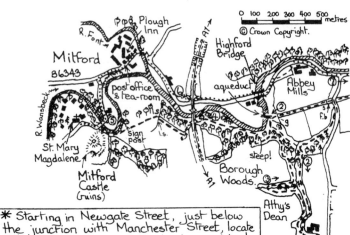

Mitford
86343

R. Font

Plough Inn

Highford Bridge

aqueduct

Abbey Mills

R. Wansbeck

post office & tea-room

St. Mary Magdalene

sign post

Mitford Castle (ruins)

steep!

Borough Woods

Athy's Dean

steps, footbridge

0 100 200 300 400 500 metres
© Crown Copyright.

* Starting in Newgate Street, just below the junction with Manchester Street, locate either Main's Terrace or Wigham's Yard. These passages let you down the bank to the Bakehouse Steps. Cross onto the Stanners.

* If the river is too high, return to Newgate St., go up to Dogger Bank, and down to the opening through to the Skinnery Bridge and onto the Stanners.......

• Skinnery Bridge is a reminder of Morpeth's old industry–tanning, using cattle from Scotland and local oak. The bridge was built in 1880 to improve recreational access to the Stanners.

(3 miles)
(5 miles).

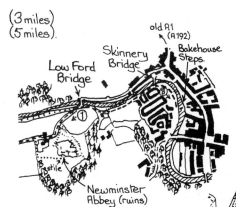

old A1 ↑ (A192)

Skinnery Bridge

Bakehouse Steps.

Low Ford Bridge

stile

Newminster Abbey (ruins)

Buses do run between Morpeth and Mitford, but not often and not every day. They are timed for schoolchildren and shoppers rather than walkers!

* .... From the High Stanners continue upriver, past the Whale-bone Arch and Skinnery Bridge, onto Lady's Walk. This is the old route to Newminster (St Mary's). It runs somewhat precariously along the bluff, undercut by the river, then turns onto a track that descends to the road just by Low Ford Bridge. Turn left here, along the hedged drive to Newminster Abbey ....

• The Whalebone Arch, in front of a house near to Skinnery Bridge, predates the house. Previously Whale-bone Cottage stood here.

• Low Ford Bridge is narrow, but strong and graceful. It dates from 1836, before the motor car, and has never come to terms with them two at a time.

✳ Newminster Abbey is private property, with no public right of access. However, the owner permits visitors to the site during the day, up to 5 p.m. You visit at your own risk, and should not touch any of the stones or ruins. Access is from the public path that goes south uphill just beyond the houses. Go up the path to beyond the hedge, where you will probably find a notice to show you where to cross the field to the south-west corner of the Abbey.

● Newminster was a large and powerful abbey, similar in style to Fountains Abbey in Yorkshire. It was a Cistercian monastery, founded in 1137 by Ranulph de Merlay. As time went by it owned land all over Northumberland. But Henry VIII sounded its death-knell in 1537, in the Dissolution of monasteries. Since then it has been thoroughly robbed of stone by the good people of Morpeth. It has been remarked that the town's beauty owes much to its stone being older than its buildings: — this is where much of it came from! Now there is little left, although much of the cloister collonade, and a couple of doorways were re-erected in 1913 following excavation. But now the elegant arches are shrouded again in brambles and ivy. Treat it with care.

* Back on the path below the Abbey, go west over a stile and across a field, keeping next to the hedge, to meet High House Road. Here there is a choice:

ⓐ go straight ahead, beside another hedge, to the riverbank, opposite the water treatment works. Go up the steps.

ⓑ go a few metres up the road, to the sign-posted path into Borough Woods. This path will take you along the foot of the beautiful woods, to the riverbank. Go up the steps between the trees to the top of the bank.

ⓒ Halfway along the Borough Woods path turn left up a sign-posted path through Athy's Dean. This path climbs through the wood, eventually crossing the burn on a foot-bridge. Continue, more muddily, on the western edge of the wood, on a zigzag contour, until you rejoin routes ⓐ and ⓑ high above the bend of the river.

A few metres along the high path you turn very steeply down to the river-bank. Carry on westwards beside the Wansbeck, and climb up beneath the utilitarian A1 viaduct. You emerge next to the carriage-way on the west side. Go on up beside a hedge to a stile. Turn right along the field-edge above the wooded banks to a ladder-stile. Down below you now is the curve of the Wansbeck, and its confluence with the Font. Mitford is on the far bank. Turn half-left and descend the bank on a long diagonal. Pass an isolated sign-post, and turn down by the rocky bank, past the Castle, to reach Fosse Bridge.

Morpeth 26: Mitford

- Mitford has shrunk in importance as Morpeth has grown. Its castle and church date back to the 12th century, founded by Sir Richard Bertram.

- The castle was built where the Wansbeck gives protection on two sides, and a burn forms a moat on the third. It was important enough to receive the royal attentions of King John in 1215, and to see off Alexander II of Scotland the year after! Edward II (England) captured it in 1316 and Alexander III wrecked it in 1318. Its value was now declining and it was allowed to decay. Now there are only the ruins of the keep, plus sections of the bailey wall.

N.B: The Castle is private property and not open to visitors.

The Mitford family returned in the reign of Charles II, but soon decamped from the castle remains to a manor house (south of the church — a ruined gateway remains). In 1830 they moved on to grander surroundings: Mitford Hall.

- The church of St. Mary Magdalene contains much 12th century work, but was so much added-to and rebuilt in the 19th century that it gives an overwhelmingly Victorian impression.

✻ From the church you can reach the village by crossing the Wansbeck over Fosse Bridge and climbing the lane to the main valley road. Turn right down the bank.

● Mitford has a post-office which doubles as a village store (soft drinks, ice-cream, biscuits...) and also has a tea-room! A little further down the hill is the Plough Inn. Buses to Morpeth are infrequent.

✻ Cross the River Font by <u>Mitford Bridge</u>, and follow the road down the valley. Wide verges and separated footways in most places mean that the infrequent traffic presents little problem. You get a very different - and worthwhile view of the attractive wooded valley from this return route.
You pass under the A1 viaduct and recross the Wansbeck by the Highford Bridge (just below the water treatment works). A field path cuts off the corner to Abbey Mills Farm, where you rejoin the road.
At Low Ford Bridge you meet your outward path. Follow it back along Lady's Walk onto the High Stanners. Cross the Bakehouse Steps, or Oldgate Bridge, and make your way into Morpeth.

✳ From the Telford Bridge in Morpeth go east past the Library along Gas House Lane. This winds down to Stob's Ford Bridge at the Low Stanners. Cross over, turn left, and follow the track out over the fields past Borehole Cottage. (Here there was a warm chalybeate spring during the last century, and bathing facilities!) Over the river you can see East Mill, that used both water and steam power over the years. It can still generate electricity from water power.

Your path goes into the edge of Quarry Woods. There were prehistoric settlements up on Waddle Bank. But you keep on near the riverside, to cross the river by the Bailey Bridge to "Woodside". Join the main road up Whorral Bank for a hundred metres or so, then escape into the woods through a gateway. A relatively new path takes you up and down among the trees, to meet the old path down the ravine.

● <u>Stobs Ford Bridge</u>, at the Low Stanners. This footbridge was originally built at the other end of town, as the Oldgate Bridge in 1872. When replaced by a roadbridge in 1931, it was towed through the town to the Low Stanners, where the ford and stepping stones were considered dangerous. Unfortunately it became stuck in Gas House Lane. It had to be cut in two, moved, then welded back together again!

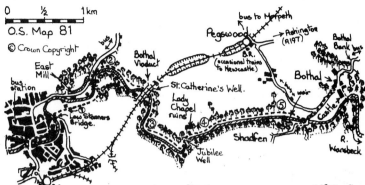

0   ½   1km
O.S. Map 81
© Crown Copyright

East Mill

bus station

Low Stannes Bridge.

Bothal Viaduct

St. Catherine's Well.

Lady Chapel ruins

Pegswood

bus to Morpeth

Ashington (A197)

B.R. (occasional trains to Newcastle)

Bothal Bank bus

Bothal

Castle

weir

Shadfen

R. Wansbeck

Jubilee Well

B.R.

• The railway viaduct is 138 ft (4.2 m) high. Completed in 1849, it carries the East Coast Main Line between Newcastle and Edinburgh, (which opened in 1847 – a temporary wooden trestle was used in the interim!).

✳ The riverside path snakes alongside the river in its wooded gorge. The river is often deep and tranquil, the woods full of wildlife. In all its moods – in the chill of a hard frost, the flowerful promise of spring, the warm glow of summer or the colourful contemplation of autumn – this woodland has much to offer.

The path passes several relics for the observant to find:

• St Catherine's Well, just past the viaduct.
• Jubilee Well (1887), 50 m before
• Our Lady's Chapel: a chantry established in the fifteenth century, and rebuilt in Victorian times, it is now ruinous.
• Lady's Well, just east of the chapel.

* The path from Bothal Woods passes a weir, then the site of Bothal Mill, to reach the Bothal - Shadfen road. [Across the bridge and up the bank a track gives access to a path back to Morpeth, high up, out of the valley — but if you do want to walk back, retracing your steps is more rewarding].
When you reach the lane, turn left. Soon you join the Pegswood – Bothal road, a pleasant avenue down into Bothal.

• Bothal has :- a Castle (NOT open to the public)
  - a Norman church
  - public conveniences
  - a 'phone box
  - a bus service to Morpeth and Ashington.

• Bothal Castle is private property, and not open to the public. Unless you are a guest of Welwyn Electrics you will have to content yourself with views from the outside. Apart from the classic view that you had as you came down the lane into Bothal the best view is from the far side of the stepping-stones. You reach them down the path between the Castle and the church.

Note that the suspension bridge is also private, as are riverside walks downstream.

• The Castle is somewhat unusual. Here is no skyline drama to remind the natives where the power lies. This site is hidden from casual view, down in the valley and not commanding any significant route. It is far enough from the cliffs to avoid arrows from over-looking besiegers. It is much more a safe family retreat than a symbol of power.

The gatehouse with its stone figures lurks behind mounds of greenery.

Technically speaking the Castle dates from 1343, when the Crown gave a licence to crenellate to Robert Bertram IV of Bothal. He was joint Sheriff of Northumberland and needed a secure house: this job created enemies! He had the gatehouse built, following the military fashion of the day, concentrating the castle's strength in one building. The curtain wall, much of which already existed, enclosed the gardens, orchards and the original manor house.

The castle's out-of-the-way location has kept it out of most of the country's turmoils, so despite periods of neglect much of the original castle survives, including the collection of royal and baronial coats of arms above the gate. There have been modifications over the centuries, of course, and a major restoration in 1831. Ownership has descended from the Bertrams and Ogles to the Duke of Portland.

Morpeth 32: St. Andrew's Church, Bothal.

St. Andrew's at Bothal is a delightful little country church, set in a yard of trees and flowers. It looks as though it just grew here, which in a way it did. There was probably a Saxon church here — parts of Saxon crosses are built into the walls. The earliest stone building was late Saxon or early Norman; perhaps where the chancel is now. But the Norman lords of Bothal had grander plans for their local church. A stone nave was built in about 1150 — parts of it still survive. At the end of the century the present chancel was built, replacing the Saxon east end, and an aisle was added on the north side, and a chapel on the south. This was extended to make a south aisle in the mid-14th century. You can try looking for evidence for all this — such as the way the south wall bends at the join, and the cutting of the old south wall to make arches between the nave and the new south aisle. Certainly the north aisle arches do not match the south! Towards the end of the 14th century the church was given new bigger windows, adding much-needed light, both in the walls and the roof.

Much later, the church was "restored" heavily in Victorian times. The evolution of the church provides much to fascinate those who like church buildings — and even those who don't will be interested, or alarmed, by the lean of the nave walls!

● Perhaps the church's most intriguing historical moment was in 1672 when the Rector was convicted for cutting the edges from silver coins and melting down the parings!

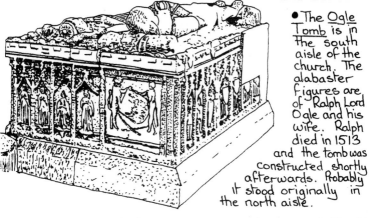

● The Ogle Tomb is in the south aisle of the church. The alabaster figures are of Ralph Lord Ogle and his wife. Ralph died in 1513 and the tomb was constructed shortly afterwards. Probably it stood originally in the north aisle.

You can see that it has been dismantled and rebuilt at some time : the side panels have been erected in the wrong order. Probably the four angels with shields stood alongside the large shield at one end, with the eight men-at-arms along one side and the four ladies (plus some missing now) along the other. See what you think! It is still magnificent!

North exterior

● <u>Sheepwash</u> was the tidal limit. Legend has it that the people of Morpeth asked a wizard to bring navigable water to Morpeth. He commanded that their best runner should race the tide up from the sea, without looking back. However, by the time he reached Sheepwash the sound of the tide behind him was so great that in fear he looked over his shoulder: so the tide stops at Sheepwash — or did, before the weir was built!

● The <u>Riverside Park</u> was created in the 1970's by the Council, replacing an almost impassable quagmire by this stretch of beautiful parkland. There are toilets, refreshments, row-boats and a play-park too, plus a camp-site.

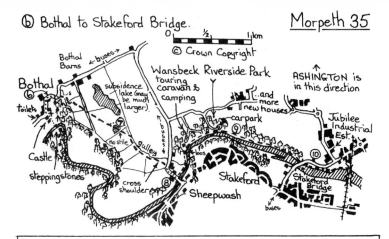

0   ½   1 km
© Crown Copyright

* There is no public access by the riverside between Bothal and Sheepwash. Climb Bothal Bank, escaping from the road -side at the sharp bend near the top. A path goes up into the fields. Follow the edge of the first above the trees over-looking Bothal. Cross the second field diagonally if you can, to reach the track from Bothal Barns. A few metres along it you pass through a gate on your left into a large pasture. You need to reach the far corner. This has been complicated by mining subsidence, which has increased the size of the pond. At the far corner you follow the hedge south-east as it dips into the depression of a field-stream, then bear right across a shoulder and drop down to meet the Sheepwash road. Go down to the bridge, and follow the riverside path eastwards through the Park.

• The railway came to North Seaton in 1859, striding across the Wansbeck on a massive wooden viaduct. That was replaced in 1927 by the present steel structure — the wooden viaduct went to make matches! The line is still busy, carrying coal from Lynemouth and Butterwell across to Cambois and Blyth, and further afield, and aluminium traffic to and from Alcan.

• The _weir_ was built as a key element in the Wansbeck Riverside Park scheme: before it was built the river below Sheepwash was rather revolting at low tide! Now it is regarded (rightly) as a valuable amenity, and the developers vie to build homes overlooking the valley.
• The mouth of the Wansbeck provides some shelter for small boats. The lockup huts house fishermen's equipment. There used to be a rope-ferry across the river here, but bridges have rendered it superfluous.

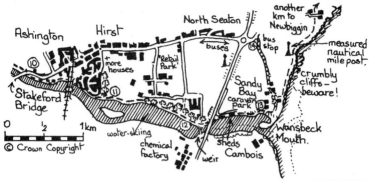

* The riverside path passes under Stakeford Bridge. Keep on, near the river, going past the huts of the Sea Scouts and on towards the railway viaduct. The path climbs up and under the viaduct, then scrambles past the garden fences of a modern estate, before descending to shore level again. The river has eaten into a Victorian rubbish tip near the old colliery: old bottles and pottery may be found sometimes on the shore.
Go on under the Northumberland Spine Road to reach Sandy Bay.

If you want to, you can catch a bus back to Morpeth from the entrance to the caravan park.

* Pick a way through the caravan park, near to the cliff edge as it rises, but not too close — the crumbly clay has been the cause of fatal accidents! You will pick up the cliff footpath as you leave the caravans behind. Note how the rock strata below you change: the black rocks indicate where this area's industrial muscle comes from (and the smoke from Cambois power station shows where some of the waste goes).

Wire fences hem in the path as you approach and pass some modern residences on the edge of the sea. Beyond, you drop down into a gulley. Either continue on the path, up the other side and straight on, or digress down to find the Needle's Eye.

If the tide permits walk along the beach, otherwise climb back over the top of the rocks to rejoin the upper path. Join the promenade for the walk round the bay towards St. Bartholomew's Church. The central section has been substantially and deeply rebuilt with new sea-defence blocks. The high sandy beach that used to protect the town disappeared, so now concrete is needed to keep the waves where they belong.

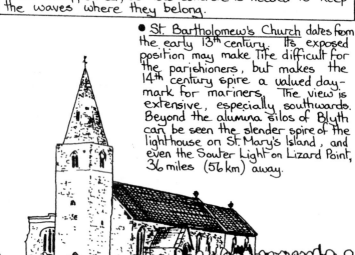

● St. Bartholomew's Church dates from the early 13th century. Its exposed position may make life difficult for the parishioners, but makes the 14th century spire a valued day-mark for mariners. The view is extensive, especially southwards. Beyond the alumina silos of Blyth can be seen the slender spire of the lighthouse on St Mary's Island, and even the Souter Light on Lizard Point, 36 miles (56 km) away.

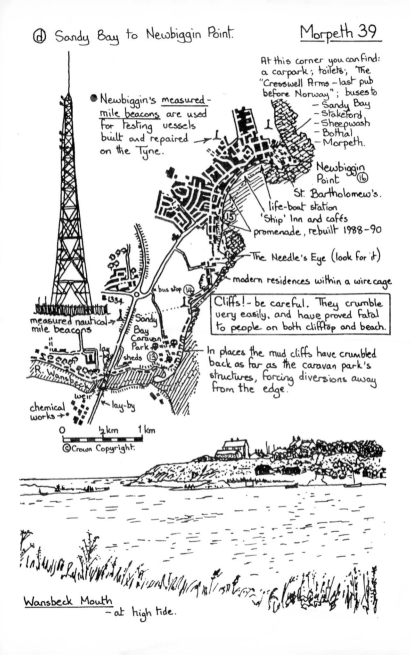

● Newbiggin's measured-mile beacons are used for testing vessels built and repaired on the Tyne.

At this corner you can find: a carpark; toilets; The "Cresswell Arms – last pub before Norway"; buses to
– Sandy Bay
– Stakeford
– Sheepwash
– Bothal
– Morpeth.

Newbiggin Point ⑯
St. Bartholomew's.
life-boat station
'Ship' Inn and cafés
promenade, rebuilt 1988–90

The Needle's Eye (look for it)

modern residences within a wire cage

measured nautical mile beacons →

B1334

⊙ bus stop ⑭

Sandy Bay Caravan Park

lay sheds ⑬

R. Wansbeck

weir   ← lay-by

chemical works →

Cliffs! – be careful. They crumble very easily, and have proved fatal to people on both clifftop and beach.

In places the mud cliffs have crumbled back as far as the caravan park's structures, forcing diversions away from the edge.

0   ½ km   1 km
© Crown Copyright.

Wansbeck Mouth
– at high tide.

Morpeth Index

ROTHBURY

Rothbury is the market town for Coquetdale. The town nestles beside the river as the valley narrows from the broad plain for the river to carve its way through the moors to the sea. All the valley traffic has to come through here. So too do the high roads over the moors from Hexham, Alnwick and Morpeth, dropping down from the heights to cross the river here. The value of this place in terms of defense, economics and agriculture, has been known for at least 3500 years, as the number of Bronze Age hillforts and settlements that overlook the town gives testimony.

But Rothbury is much more than a good site. Its people have made the most of this place, making it a town with its own distinctive — and lovely — style.

Front Street — central Rothbury!

Rothbury 2

CENTRAL ROTHBURY
(NOT to scale).

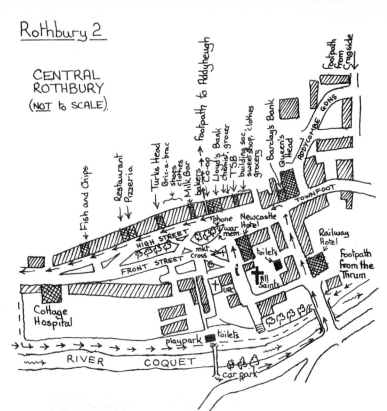

Transport: Buses operate to and from Morpeth daily, and to and from Newcastle on weekdays. In summer buses go via the Cragside entrance to Alnwick.
Post buses operate up the valley on weekdays (infrequently), and others run now and then to Otterburn.

Car Parking: High Street and Front Street quickly become clogged with parked cars. There is a carpark beside the river, on the opposite bank, from where a footbridge and footpath give quick access to the town.

Contents

---

* A sensible place to start is at the Information Centre. This is in the Council Offices, between the Newcastle Hotel and All Saints Church. It has informative displays.

• <u>All Saints Church</u>, next door, is a dignified Victorian rebuild and extension of a 13th century church. You can still see the early building in the chancel and transepts. Even older is the stem of the font: under the 1664 bowl the carved stem is part of the shaft of an Anglo-Saxon cross. The Ascension scene is thought to be the oldest of its kind in England. Other parts of the cross — the head, and more of the shaft — are in the Black Gate museum in Newcastle.

The church shows the patronage of the Armstrongs in its interior woodwork — the chancel screen and pulpit. The family have their burial plot outside — they really did make Rothbury their home.

• The <u>market cross</u> is twentieth century. Erected by the townspeople, it commemorates the first Lord and Lady Armstrong.

* Cross the green to High Street, and walk up the bank to the head of the town.

• High Street (together with Townfoot) is the shopping centre for upper Coquetdale. The town has all the commercial facilities you would expect of a prospering rural market town.
What sets it apart is the green, with its magnificent trees. This transforms it from an ordinary, dour Northern town to a place of delight.

Turk's Head.

Rothbury 6 : Riverside

● Coquet Lodge, the imposing building at the top of the town, is the Cottage (!) Hospital, where many Northumbrians have come for recuperation and convalescence.

> ✱ Just beyond, turn down to the riverside : a steep path goes down by the wall, or a gentler route from the carpark. Turn back along the riverside path, below the town, to a children's playpark. Cross the footbridge to the carpark. Walk along the verge to the road-bridge, cross over and walk back into the town.

● Rothbury Bridge is an amalgam of ancient and modern, with a new deck on the old arches. The basis was a 16th century packhorse Bridge, which had to be widened when the Corn Laws caused a massive export drive. The Corn Road was built between Hexham and Alnmouth in 1753.

Rothbury Bridge

• Rothbury has its fair share of inns and public houses, as you would expect in a market town. The Railway Hotel, at the north end of the bridge, is a reminder that Rothbury used to have a railway. This started out as a grandiose scheme for a new Anglo-Scottish route, the Northumberland Central Railway. In reality it was a single-track branch line from Scots-gap and Morpeth. It closed to passengers in 1952, and to goods in 1963.

The Queens Head and the Turks Head have impressive painted signs. Less obvious are the old signs built in: the Queens Head on the wall; the Turks Head up on the edge of the roof.

Rothbury 8 : Walk to Cragside, by the Carriage Drive.

Note: Cragside and its grounds are National Trust properties and charge an entrance fee for non-members. An alternative route avoiding Cragside is offered for the impecunious.

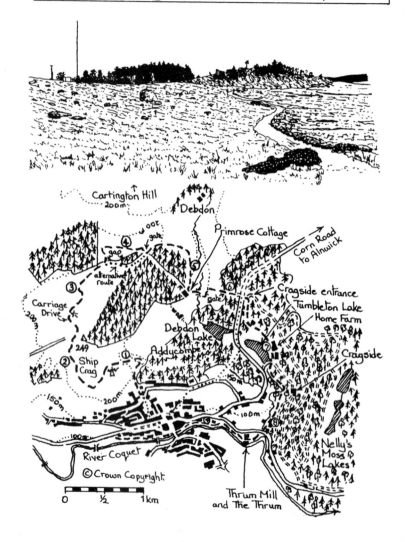

Cartington Hill 200m

Debdon

Primrose Cottage

Corn Road to Alnwick

moor

gate

gap

alternative route

Carriage Drive

Cragside entrance

Tumbleton Lake

Home Farm

gate

Debdon Lake

Addycombe

Ship Crag

Cragside

150m

200m

100m

Nelly's Moss Lakes

River Coquet

© Crown Copyright

0   ½   1km

Thrum Mill and The Thrum

✱ Leave the High Street by the alley beside the Co-op. At the first road go briefly left, then up the right hand of a pair of drive-ways. Steps lead up to another cross-road. Go straight up to a stile that gives onto open moorland next to the wood.

Follow the path up until you reach the Carriage Drive. Turn left along it, down into the Coplish Burn basin, then winding up past the Rothbury television mast and Ship Crag. Enjoy the views up Coquetdale, and across the river to the dark skyline of the Simonsides.

Keep on pretending that you are in the Armstrong family carriage as you follow the drive northwards along the rim of the moor, towards Cartington Hill. As you turn east a gap in the wall offers a chance to walk along the ridge beyond. (If your navigation skills are poor stay on the Drive). You rejoin the Drive where it crosses the Cartington track, and follow it round the edge of the wood to Primrose Cottage.

Here you have to leave the Drive (the rest is private) and follow the rough road east to the Corn Road. The entrance to Cragside is immediately opposite.

Primrose Cottage

✱ At the gate of Cragside you have to make a decision. If you are a National Trust member you will naturally exercise your privileges and choose the scenic route through the grounds, and back to Rothbury via the Thrum. But if you are not a member, and are not intending to visit the house or other parts of the grounds, you may think the entrance fee excessive for pursuing this walk. There is an alternative route (below) - or you could consider joining the National Trust.

✱ Cheap alternative route back to Rothbury
Follow the Corn Road (B6341) downhill to the bridge between Debdon Lake and Tumbleton Lake. Just beyond, turn right up a fenced footpath onto the ridge. At the crest you cross a private section of the Carriage Drive, and have a superb view over the town to the Simonsides.
 A green footpath goes down diagonally across the meadows straight towards the town. At Hillside Road turn right for 600 metres, then turn down another field path to Addycombe Gardens on the edge of town.

Down to Rothbury

Tumbleton Lake

---

* Main route:
Follow the drive down towards the Home Farm, or turn
off onto the quiet track that winds round the west
side of Tumbleton Lake.

• The Home Farm is now the Visitors' Centre, with a café
to refresh the body, an energy exhibition to excite the
imagination, and a shop to deplete the purse.

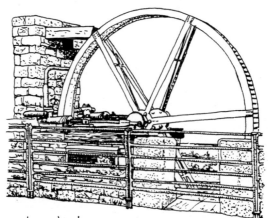

• A working water-wheel
driving a hydraulic pump, erected
in the stable yard — just one of many exhibits.

Rothbury 12 : Cragside

● Cragside is a monument to the Industrial Revolution. Its builder was that inventive engineer, William Lord Armstrong. He used some of the money from his Tyneside engineering industry to create Cragside. In 1863 this was a bare, rocky hillside. The house, the lakes and the seven million trees are typical of his innovative energy. When fellow Tynesider Joseph Swan found how to use electricity for lighting, Lord Armstrong made this one of the first houses in the land to be electrically lit, using his own hydro-electric generating plant on the estate. Other machinery in the house and farm was powered hydraulically, using water from high-up Nelly's Moss Lakes.

The first house was not imposing enough for the new setting, and after twenty years Lord Armstrong had it enlarged substantially, resulting in the magnificent (if rather bizarre) Gothic schloss that we now see. It is worth a visit. If you do not have the time now, come back! Not only are the family rooms impressive, but the kitchens too: Armstrong used his industrial expertise here as well, with powered appliances for the staff to use.

The energy exhibition in the Visitors' Centre is well-worth visiting. It is informative, interesting and well-presented. It is complemented by the "Power Circuit", a trail around the house and grounds that draws attention to power sources and the way that energy is used.

But Lord Armstrong's genius was not just with the mechanical. The estate around the house is finely laid out with drives and walks. These too are worth a return visit. In late spring thousands of azaleas and rhododendrons splash the hillside with colour. The pinetum below the house, with its mature trees, is awe-inspiring in its own right.

Leaflets describing all these, in more detail, are available from the Visitors' Centre.

Cragside is in the care of the National Trust.
Car-borne visitors must enter by the Debdon Gate.
Tickets for the grounds and for the House can be obtained at the Debdon gate or at the House.

Rothbury 14 Debdon Gorge.

> * From the Visitors' Centre go down the drive towards the cross-roads. A footpath sign-posted "The Power Circuit" leads down steps to the Pump-House, then down the gorge to the Power House.

On the way there is much to see:

● The Pump House. A ram pump uses hydraulic power from Tumbleton Lake to force water up the hill to the Basin Tank above the House.

● The Rustic Bridge, in wood, is a copy of one built by Lord Armstrong in the 1870's.

● The slender and elegant Iron Bridge is not actually made of Iron! It is one of the earliest bridges made of steel. It was produced in the Armstrong works at Elswick on the Tyne, in the early 1870's.
(The path does not cross the Iron Bridge, but ducks underneath)

● The pinetum shows just how beautiful conifers can be given space and attention.

● Ivy Bridge (below) and the gorge. There was a mill here once. Can you spot the pit for the water-wheel and its tail-race, cut into the rock?

● The Power House (1886) contains the hydro-electric generator first used to provide electricity for the House, plus the back-up gas-powered generator.

* You can leave the Cragside estate by continuing along the path beyond the Power House. You reach the Rothbury to Weldon Bridge road (B6344) at Burnfoot Lodge.

Rothbury 16: The Thrum

● <u>The Thrum</u>, where the whole river Coquet gushes through a narrow cleft in a band of harder rock. It is spectacular, and noisy, when the river is full. Like the Strid (on the Wharfe in Yorkshire) the Thrum has seen many young folk dared to jump across the gap. After some fatalities the Thrum was widened with dynamite to discourage attempts.

* Turn right from Burnfoot Lodge, and cross the Debdon Burn by the stone road-bridge. Cross the road and follow the track beside the river Coquet.
In just a few metres this brings you to the Thrum, and, just beyond, to Thrum Mill.

• Just above Thrum Mill sits a little hut on the riverbank, with a wire and pulley arrangement stretching out across the river to the trees on the far bank. What is it for? Let your imagination work a bit. Is it for eel lines? It is surely not for salmon nets! Is it for ducking witches? Does Rothbury boast a wire-walker who uses this for practice? The answer, when your mind stops boggling, is on the bibliography page at the end of the book!

* Continue by the riverside. The access-road to the mill and cottages turns right to the road, but a footpath continues along wooded banks by a delightful stretch of river that twists and turns towards Rothbury. Pass a set of stepping stones and go on towards the bridge. A depth gauge on the side of the bridge is a reminder that the river is not always a benign companion.

* Make your way to the riverside (by footpaths next to All Saints or the United Reformed Church) and follow it westwards below the town gardens. Soon you leave the town behind and cross the Golf Club access road (NOT its bridge!) South of the river here is the old Rothbury Racecourse, closed in 1966 despite local opposition.

You touch the road briefly (unless you fight through the vegetation), then a gate leads onto a footpath through gorse and scrub on a bank above a bend in the river.

After a boggy section the path heads across the meadow, over a stile and on to <u>Lady's Bridge</u> (below).

The track beyond develops into a muddy lane, that suddenly turns up to Newtown Mills. Here Coquetdale plaids used to be woven, until the family died out. Continue up the track past the houses, and bear left to a road junction. Turn right up the avenue to Great Tosson.

At the junction by the Peel Tower go along to the right, past the farm.

● <u>Great Tosson Peel Tower</u> is one of many in Northumberland. In the mediaeval period this was a lawless land, and residents needed a tower to retire into when the Reivers came a'raiding. This one has been 'peeled' of dressed stones at its bottom.

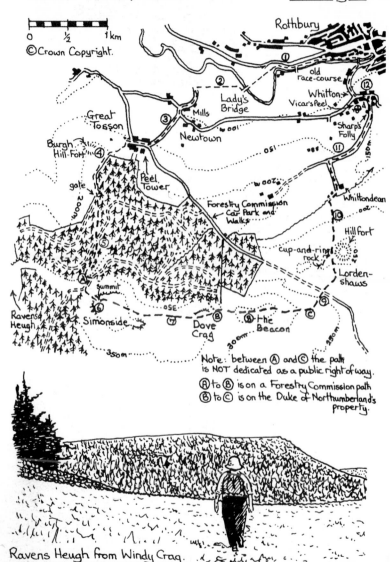

12.6 km (8 miles) circular.

© Crown Copyright.

Rothbury

old race-course

Whitton
Vicar's Peel

Lady's Bridge

Mills

Great Tosson

Newtown

Sharp's Folly

Burgh Hill-Fort

gate

Peel Tower

Forestry Commission Car Park and Walks

Whittondean

Hill fort

cup-and-ring rock

Lorden-shaws

summit

Ravens Heugh

Simonside

Dove Crag

the Beacon

Note: between Ⓐ and Ⓒ the path is NOT dedicated as a public right of way.

Ⓐ to Ⓑ is on a Forestry Commission path

Ⓑ to Ⓒ is on the Duke of Northumberland's property.

Ravens Heugh from Windy Crag.

* At the west end of Great Tosson do not turn down the hill, but go on briefly along the track. Once past the farmyard turn uphill. A footpath slants across Slatebrae to the forest corner.

● Burgh Hill, on your right, is one of many Bronze Age hill-forts in the area.

* The path continues up the hill-side over Windy Crag. Ravens Heugh pops into view ahead, then Simonside appears above the trees. At a gate (left) enter the forest. You soon meet a forest track. Cross straight over and continue uphill. At the next forest track you meet the red and orange way-marks of the Forestry Commission.

Their route joins our path on its diagonal slope up between the trees. But it is not just trees: rocks, bracken, bilberries and wildlife engage your interest on the gentle climb.

* As you emerge from the top of the forest the red and orange routes veer off to the left. Follow them (it is easier!) Stick with the red route when they split. It goes across the heather and joins another forestry track below the ramparts of Simonside (below left). There are many ways up for the adventurous (this is the nursery for Northumberland's rock-climbers), but the red route is easy: along the forestry track to the west of the top, then up beside a huge boulder to avoid the crags.
Climb up to the summit (above) and enjoy the extensive view of Upper Coquetdale and the Cheviots.

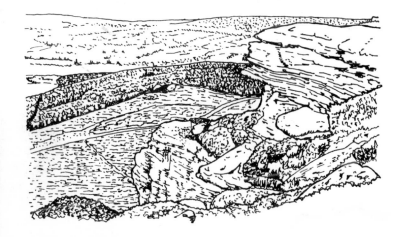

* Follow the Forestry Commission red route eastwards across the almost level top of Simonside towards the shattered rocks of the east top: Little Simonside. The red route boggily bypasses the rocks on their north side and dips down across the col towards Dove Crag. If the weather is clear you can spot landmarks along the Northumberland coast.

* From Dove Crag the Forestry red route goes its own way, dipping down to the corner of the wood, to return to the car park.

* The path on across the Beacon is also not dedicated as a right of way, but has been used by walkers for very many years. It crosses the property of the Duke of Northumberland.

Beyond the Beacon the path continues along the same line, running alongside the broken remains of a wall until it joins the public path from Spylaw. This goes down to cross the road.

Continue in the same direction, heading to pass between the two hillocks. Go through the gate in the fence, and watch for a grassy path turning up left to a large boulder on the south shoulder of the hillock.

● <u>Lordenshaws</u> : the large cup-and-ring marked rock is one of several on this hill. The Bronze Age markings must have had great significance in their time, but their meaning is now obscure. Are they fertility symbols, maps of the local hill forts and burial mounds, or epitaphs? The hillside also has burial cists and a stone alignment. On its summit is a good example of a Bronze Age hill-fort, with encircling ditches and earth ramparts. This was a place of importance 3500 years ago.

* Half-way between the large cup-and-ring rock and the hill-fort a fragment of wall shows where the footpath to Rothbury goes. Follow the yellow waymarks carefully as it dips northwards down the hillside. It goes down through bracken (beware of adders) into the valley of Whitton Burn. The path goes through a gate beside the burn, at the corner of a wood. Go past the pond and follow the track up left, across the burn to the Whittondean farmhouse. A wooden gate next to the house shows the way across the garden to another gate. Follow the farm access lane northwards, turning right onto Hillhead road to follow the curving ridge down towards Rothbury.

● Sharp's Folly is the prominent round tower plainly in view next to the caravan and camping park. The rector of Rothbury, Dr Sharp, had it built as an observatory in about 1720. Before the trees blocked it there was a view to the sea as well as the stars.

* Continue down the lane. Keep left through Whitton, and descend the leafy lane to a road junction

● Whitton Tower, amongst the trees on the left at the junction, was the Rothbury Rectory. Its heart is a 14th century Peel Tower, extended to provide greater comfort in more peaceful times. (It is not open to the public).

* From the road junction follow the signpost for Rothbury, and walk down the road. There is an ample verge to cushion tired feet for most of the way.
The footbridge provides a quick way over the river into the town.

Rothbury Index

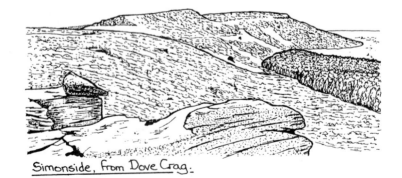

Simonside, from Dove Crag.

intermission: Rothbury to Warkworth.

The Coquet between these two towns is at its best. The river snakes down the valley, full of picturesque bends and clothed with beautiful trees. It is just how a river should be.

Unfortunately the same cannot be said for the riverside footpaths. Mainly because they do not exist! For long stretches of river there are no riverside paths at all. The ancients who made the original tracks quite sensibly steered clear of the bogs and rampant vegetation. They made good straightish paths well up the valley sides, where drainage was better and enemies more easily spotted. These more direct paths were shorter too, cutting off the deep loops of the meandering river. So — few riverside paths for twentieth century romantics!

However, if you can be content to enjoy the really good spots, between long stretches of fairly mediocre field- or even road-walking, you can attempt to walk between Rothbury and Warkworth, beside the Coquet.

Paths are not good in many places, and way-marking (at the time of writing) is minimal or less. There are serious obstructions in places that may cause you to choose an alternative to the close-to-river route — such as the lack of a footbridge over the Coquet at Morwick Mill!

But if this has not put you off, and you are determined to link these two towns, the following notes may help. DO USE OS 1:25000 maps to help your detailed route-finding, to keep you on the bent and narrow way.

(If you already have the National Park guide, "Walks in Coquetdale", you will find details of the flora to be seen on the Rothbury to Felton section — and 1:25000 maps!)

The complete walk is long, 32 kilometres, and is best tackled in sections, using buses to return you to your starting point (or to take you there!).

Intermission 2 : Rothbury to Pauperhaugh.

There are two routes, one above each bank:

✱ On the north bank the better, more picturesque route has been appropriated by the road, which is winding, footpath-less and heavily trafficked in summer. The first kilometre or so is the delightful riverbank path to Thrum Mill, but beyond that the road is unavoidable. It would be wonderful without the cars! It is good by bus!

✱ On the southern bank is a path put together by the Northumberland National Park and Countryside Department. You leave Rothbury over the bridge, and turn left up the Hexham road. Turn off left along Mill Lane, and walk along for a kilometre, with fine views over the Thrum to the Cragside Woods. When you reach the old railway, turn right along it.......

The Rothbury to Scots Gap railway was a North British Railway venture, another of their plans to link England and Scotland without benefit of the North-Eastern Railway along the coast. This plan came to a halt at Rothbury, but it was a well-used branch line until motor traffic made it redundant. It closed in 1963.

©Crown Copyright.

✱ .... The railway line is a permissive path. (That means you may WALK along it, courtesy of the owner, not indulge in permissive activities) It replaces the overgrown and difficult public footpath that gets lost east of Wagtail Farm. Play trains for another kilometre. You pass through a cutting that has (at the time of writing) a rickety footbridge over the top. Just beyond, near a gate, a waymarked stile shows where the path sets off down the fields to pass Craghead cottage......

✻ .... East of Craghead cottage the path contours across the fields, through a series of gates, with the pastures falling away on the left down to the river. Continue to West Row.

Turn right, following the track then the road to a junction where a road comes down the hill from the right. You turn LEFT, through a gate, and walk beside the hedge to pass round a cottage. Turn left here, through a gate, and head for the big curving hedge. Go through a gate on your left so that the big hedge ends up on your right.

Follow the curve of the hedge, and descend into the little side-valley, turning left to a wicket gate before you reach the bottom. Go through the plantation and cross the little bridge beyond the next gate. Walk down to the river. You can actually walk beside it for a few metres, before heading directly for the gate beside Pauperhaugh Bridge

Pauperhaugh Bridge

Intermission 4: Pauperhaugh to Weldon Bridge.

✳ From Pauperhaugh Bridge walk south along the lane, for almost ½ km. A footbridge on the left carries you over the burn. Turn back northwards, round the base of the hillside, to a stile. Cross it and walk along with the fence on your right initially, to reach the Coquet again.

For half a kilometre you can walk alongside the river and its trees. If you are lucky you may see a heron. Ahead of you the riverside bluffs rise up to Thorneyhaugh, and you too climb up away from the river to the farm.

Turn left past the wall in front of the farmhouse, and pass through a gate. The footpath goes eastwards down the bank, parallel to the wood, to a bridge over the Maglin burn. The way up the east bank is not obvious until you breast the rise, and can see the gate in the next dip. Head towards the farm of Middleheugh, where you cross the road and the bog in front of the stile opposite.

The path goes left round the field edge, and up the edge of the plantation.

Out of sight, except for occasional glimpses through the foliage, Brinkburn Priory sits on the loop in the river, below the trees. You cannot reach it from this side. Visit it another day, or walk back from Weldon Bridge!

Follow the plantation round to the farm of Brinkheugh, then go along the farm road for a kilometre, passing three times under the power lines. A gate on the left opens onto a footpath that leads to the Thistleyhaugh road. Turn right towards a cottage, but go through a gate before you get to it, go round behind it and follow the hedge eastwards. Descend to a footbridge over the Tod Burn. A riverside path in the woods leads to Weldon Bridge.

● Brinkburn Priory is tucked away out of sight on a
loop of the river. It can hardly be seen from the south,
due to the cliffs and woods, and the valley road on
the north bank passes it by without a glimpse. This is
not accidental: when the Border reivers and Scots
raiding parties were at large the first line of defence
was concealment. Nevertheless it too often did not
succeed — tradition holds that a too-early ringing of
the bells in thanks for deliverance once called the Scots
back to wreak havoc. Certainly the priory became an
impoverished house by the time of its dissolution in
1552. The church buildings continued in parish use, and
although they became ruinous, enough remained to allow
the superb 1858 restoration to reproduce it in its 12th
and 13th century elegance and simplicity.
Now it is in the care of English Heritage, and is certainly
a place to visit — from the north bank!

Intermission 6 : Weldon Bridge to Felton

Don't give up here — this is the best section.

If you walk this as a single section note that buses from Morpeth serve both start and finish.

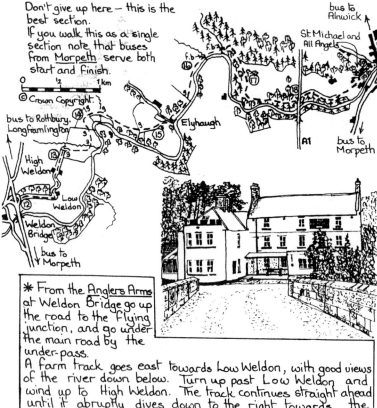

* From the Anglers Arms at Weldon Bridge go up the road to the flying junction, and go under the main road by the under-pass.

A farm track goes east towards Low Weldon, with good views of the river down below. Turn up past Low Weldon and wind up to High Weldon. The track continues straight ahead until it abruptly dives down to the right towards the river. Before it gets there the path curves northwards and passes through two gates. Now it heads for the top of the hillside again, climbing up away from the river to gain a ridge that cuts the corner towards Elyhaugh.

Cross the lane and go through a gate just left of the house. A burn leads you down to a lovely stretch of the Coquet. Follow the path north-eastwards, at first in the trees next to the river, then cutting the corner. Continue towards the bridge over Swarland Burn.

Climb up to the right and follow tracks through the fine woodland, high above the river in its gorge, to the viaduct.

● The 30 metre high viaduct carries the bustling traffic of the main road to Scotland. This bypass opened in 1981, allowing Felton to return to a quiet existence free from traffic.

*.... The footpath passes under the A1 viaduct, and climbs back up on the east side to a convenient seat. Continue through beautiful woods, high above the river, and emerge into Felton Park. Contour along, joining the drive, to the public road at St. Michael's Church. Turn right down the hill to the Swarland road, and round the corner to Felton Bridge.

● St Michael and All Angels, Felton, looks to have lost its roof as you approach. It hasn't, but the nave roof is unusually flat, whereas the chancel is high-peaked. A massive porch and bellcot add to its arresting appearance. It dates back to the 13th century, with later additions and alterations. It is an interesting place, worth a visit.

● Felton, as the bridging point on the Great North Road, saw the passing-by of much history. King John burnt it in 1216 after the Northumbrian barons paid homage to Alexander of Scotland.

Intermission 8 : Felton to Morwick Mill

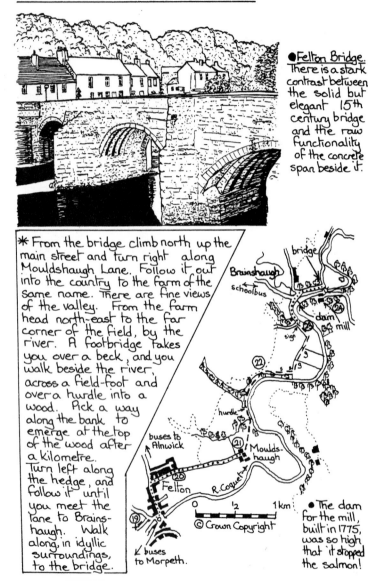

● Felton Bridge. There is a stark contrast between the solid but elegant 15th century bridge and the raw functionality of the concrete span beside it.

✳ From the bridge climb north up the main street and turn right along Mouldshaugh Lane. Follow it out into the country to the farm of the same name. There are fine views of the valley. From the farm head north-east to the far corner of the field, by the river. A footbridge takes you over a beck, and you walk beside the river, across a field-foot and over a hurdle into a wood. Pick a way along the bank to emerge at the top of the wood after a kilometre. Turn left along the hedge, and follow it until you meet the lane to Brainshaugh. Walk along, in idyllic surroundings, to the bridge.

bridge

Brainshaugh

← schoolbus

dam

mill

sign

22

hurdle

buses to ↑ Alnwick

21 Mouldshaugh

20 Felton

R. Coquet

0   ½   1km

© Crown Copyright

19

↙ buses to Morpeth.

● The dam for the mill, built in 1775, was so high that it stopped the salmon!

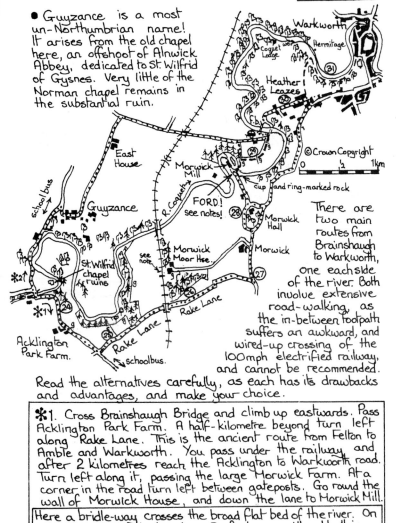

● Guyzance is a most un-Northumbrian name! It arises from the old chapel here, an offshoot of Alnwick Abbey, dedicated to St. Wilfrid of Gysnes. Very little of the Norman chapel remains in the substantial ruin.

© Crown Copyright

There are two main routes from Brainshaugh to Warkworth, one each side of the river. Both involve extensive road-walking, as the in-between footpath suffers an awkward, and wired-up crossing of the 100mph electrified railway, and cannot be recommended.

Read the alternatives carefully, as each has its drawbacks and advantages, and make your choice.

✱1. Cross Brainshaugh Bridge and climb up eastwards. Pass Acklington Park Farm. A half-kilometre beyond turn left along Rake Lane. This is the ancient route from Felton to Amble and Warkworth. You pass under the railway and after 2 kilometres reach the Acklington to Warkworth road. Turn left along it, passing the large Morwick Farm. At a corner in the road turn left between gateposts. Go round the wall of Morwick House, and down the lane to Morwick Mill.

Here a bridle-way crosses the broad flat bed of the river. On a horse you might stay dry. On foot you will not! It is a venture only for warm summer days when you can see the bottom. If in doubt, don't! – you can always go back up to the road and walk safely along to Heather Leazes.

✱1 (continued) From the bridle-way ford opposite Morwick Mill climb the track beside the conifer plantation, and turn right through a gate. A field-path contours round the hillside, matching the meander of the Coquet, to meet a tarmac road. Go down towards the ford (for cars this time), and follow the footpath along the near bank, next to the caravan park, to the long footbridge. This crossing you can do dry! The path rejoins the lane. Climb up into the pleasant suburbia of Heather Leazes. At a T-junction you meet the route of those who showed good sense at Morwick Mill and went round by road! Turn left, and follow the track past Howlet Hall and down to the riverside opposite Warkworth Hermitage (see Warkworth pages 20 to 23). Follow the beautiful riverside path into Warkworth.

<u>Upstream from the long footbridge.</u>

✱2 From Brainshaugh Bridge turn north along the road past the chapel field and beside the river. Climb up to a T-junction, where turn sharp right through the hamlet of Guyzance. Follow the road for 1½ kilometres across the plateau past East House. Turn right at another T, then keep straight on when the road turns left. Go down over a level crossing to the Morwick peninsula, where you join ✱1 for the footbridge.

warkworth

Warkworth town displays the essential characteristics
of this border kingdom: a defensive position; a river;
a castle and a quiet elegance largely unravaged by
English commercialism.
This is a town to enjoy in any season — when a hard frost
bites as the sun sinks behind black skeletons of trees
beneath an apricot-coloured sky, or when balmy breezes
shake the leaves above your rowing boat on a summer day.
Warkworth is Northumbrian.
Warkworth is romantic!

Warkworth 2

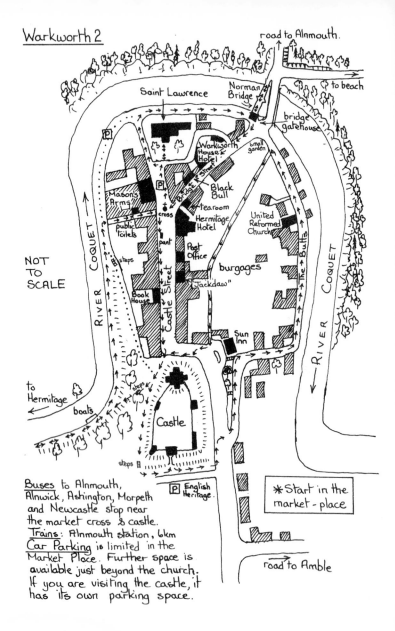

road to Alnmouth.

to beach

Saint Lawrence

Norman Bridge

bridge gatehouse

small garden

Warkworth House Hotel

Bridge Street

Black Bull

tearoom

Mason's Arms

cross

Hermitage Hotel

United Reformed Church

public toilets

pant

Post Office

burgages

The Butts

steps

Castle Street

"Jackdaw"

RIVER COQUET

Book House

NOT TO SCALE

RIVER COQUET

Sun Inn

to Hermitage

steps

boats

Castle

steps

P English Heritage.

Buses to Alnmouth, Alnwick, Ashington, Morpeth and Newcastle stop near the market cross & castle.

Trains: Alnmouth station, 6km

Car Parking is limited in the Market Place. Further space is available just beyond the church. If you are visiting the castle, it has its own parking space.

road to Amble

*Start in the market-place

Contents

Warkworth Castle

Warkworth 4 : Saint Lawrence.

As long ago as 737 AD. there was a church of St. Lawrence in Warkworth, but their building was probably destroyed by Danish raids in the ninth century.

A stone church was built — its foundations underlie today's chancel arch. The nave of the present building is Norman. Its function was to protect the people physically as well as spiritually. Note the rather forbidding north wall, with its few, high-set windows. Nevertheless the population, three hundred in all, were massacred in the church during a Scots raid in 1174 AD.

The west tower was added around 1200 AD.

The Percy family extended the church in the fifteenth century, adding the south aisle. This made the church much lighter and brighter, if less secure. (But now the castle was much stronger).

A detailed guide to the church building can be bought inside for a small sum: its purchase may help to keep the fabric up for another nine hundred years.

A peaceful winter evening; St Lawrence.

The <u>chancel arch</u> is a typical Norman semi-circular arch, decorated, and now slightly askew.

Beyond is the <u>Norman chancel</u>, with beautiful vaulting, of a style developed in Durham Cathedral.

The chancel contains parts of early <u>Celtic crosses</u> from the early days of the church.

Near the door is a <u>tomb</u> with the effigy of a knight upon it. The inscription suggests that Sir Hugh died in the Crusades, but the style of armour suggests otherwise. The shield carries the arms of the de Aublyn family of Durham.

> * After visiting the church go back out of the churchyard and follow the wall to the right, to the riverside, and along to the bridge.

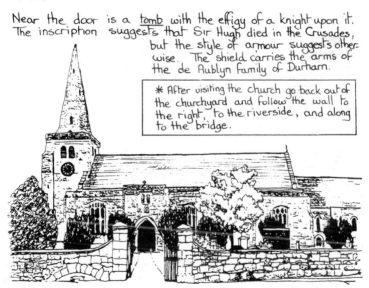

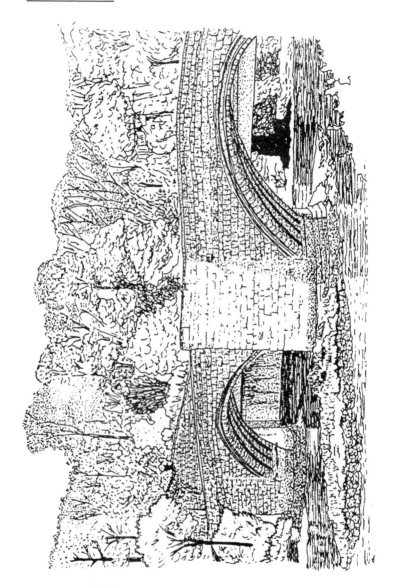

The <u>bridge</u> is a widened version of the Norman bridge.
A cross used to stand in the eastern refuge, until it was thrown into the river by "certain idle persons" in 1830. Vandalism is nothing new! Until the new bridge was built alongside, in 1965, all the traffic had to negotiate the gatehouse and narrow bridge. Bus driving must have been interesting!

The <u>gatehouse</u> is most unusual.
Very few towns in England have a fortified bridge. This one was necessary to secure the defensive position of the castle from attack at this point of weakness. It includes a lockup cell, used until not long ago to confine persons arrested for being drunk and disorderly.

Warkworth 8 : Bridge Street

✳ From the gatehouse by the bridge walk into town along Bridge Street to the Market Place.

Bridge Street presents a dour face to arrivals from the north. The dark houses open directly onto the narrow street. It looks and feels rather like a gauntlet to be run to reach the centre of town.

Warkworth has five hostelries to cater to the needs of market visitors but also for travellers. Note the openings through into court-yards for stabling. Here horses would be changed for journeys on to Alnwick or Morpeth.
Today's travellers also find a welcome.

Warkworth Inns:

- Warkworth House Hotel (top)
- The Black Bull (above).
- The Hermitage Hotel (right)
- The Mason's Arms (next page)
- The Sun Inn, at the other end of town, next to the castle.

Right here, in 1715, James "the Pretender" was proclaimed as King in England for the first time, at the start of the Jacobite rebellion. The army paused here on its way round Northumberland, recruiting for the Catholic cause, and joined here a party from Scotland. The vicar refused to conduct worship for them, and rode off to inform the authorities in Newcastle.

The Market Cross, (below), dates from 1830. It replaced an earlier cross, dating from 1706, the base and stump of which are now in the castle. The cross is a reminder to traders that God is active in the market-place as well as in the church.

Market Cross and Castle Street

Warkworth 10 : Castle Street

✳ From the market-place walk up the hill towards the castle.

Castle Street is distinctly lighter in tone than Bridge Street. It is wider and more open, to accommodate the market, and it gets the sun more. The trees add their touch of cheer too.

This part of the village has escaped the horrors of high-street modernism and retains its plain Northumbrian style.

The <u>pant</u> (right) is an essential feature for any market. It is inactive at present.

To a passing motorist the village appears to offer little by way of normal commercial facilities. This is partly due to the lack of "standard" shopfronts.

Those on foot can find   (at the time of writing)

- — a bank
- — a post-office
- — two café/tea-rooms
- — two general stores
- — an antiques shop
- — a gift/crafts shop
- — a bookshop (see below)
- — five inns   (already mentioned)
- — two churches   (St. Lawrence, Church of England, (United Reformed — on the Butts).
- — public toilets   (in Hotspur Court, near the market place).
- — an art gallery.

What more can you require?

In spring the castle motte at the head of Castle Street is a riot of golden daffodils. — much better than Grasmere.

The Book House (right) deserves a special mention, as the home of Sandhill Press. Call in and buy something — preferably another of the author's works!

* Go round outside the curtain wall of the castle, on the west side. A surfaced footpath (with steps up) takes you to the gatehouse where you can decide whether to visit the interior. English Heritage is custodian of the castle, and makes a charge for visits. They also publish an excellent detailed guidebook.

There had to be a castle at Warkworth. It is on the coastal road, with convenient harbour facilities, and there was that superb defensive position — the horseshoe loop of the river. A mound at the south end closed the ring.
The castle that you see is built up on the original mound, (motte) and courtyard (bailey). The keep is positioned to give the best views up and down-river, and the main street of the town was built under its direct gaze, with the approach from the south-east curving round the bailey.

The curtain walls that surround the bailey date in part from the twelfth century, and, oddly, do not enclose the whole of the original bailey. The castle was strengthened during the twelfth to fifteenth centuries, with further towers, living quarters, a new keep..... It was a notable factor in the struggles between English and Scots.

In 1332 the castle was granted by Edward III to Henry, second Lord Percy of Alnwick. Since then its history has been closely entwined with that of the Northumberland Percys, who for a while chose this as their main residence in preference to Alnwick. Even now they maintain a presence in the keep.

The Percys, including the famous Harry Hotspur who did not live to inherit the Earldom, were pivotal characters in the turbulent times at the start of the fifteenth century. The first Earl, and his son Hotspur, were largely responsible for settling Henry IV on England's throne, and then were instrumental in various attempts to unseat him! Thus Warkworth is the setting for three scenes in William Shakespeare's "Henry the Fourth, Part One". Considering that the Percys had made it both secure and remarkably comfortable, the reference to it as "that worm-eaten hold of ragged stone" was peculiarly inaccurate!

<u>West Postern.</u>

to gate-house

to river

Warkworth 14 : the Castle

The gatehouse is massively impressive. Built in the 13th century it is a superb piece of design and construction. Originally there was a draw-bridge: you can see where it fitted up against the gate. Up above are large square holes where the timber galleries were fitted. From these archers, rock-throwers and oil-boilers could fire down on attackers. Even if the enemy passed the gate and portcullis they found out the hard way that there was a second gate, with plenty of nooks for well-protected defenders to add to their misery!

The Lion Tower sports the remains of a splendid Percy Lion, and two coats of arms. Note the Percy crescent with the motto 'Esperance' around the lion's neck. The tower forms an entrance to the Great Hall, the main domestic building.

In the centre of the bailey are the foundations of a Collegiate church, an idea of the first Earl who wanted a college of secular canons here. It was never completed.

The keep is a lovely piece of military architecture, combining strength, defendability and comfort for the occupants together with elegance of shape. (Did you notice the rampant Percy Lion on the face overlooking the town?)

From the keep you can reverse the fine river views, looking downstream to Amble and Coquet Island, and up towards the Hermitage (not itself visible). There is a marvelous view over the town and its burgages. On the south side you look out over the bailey, the curtain walls and other towers, such as the Grey Mare's Tail Tower (below). Can you find the tiny carved crucifixes in this tower?

* Make your way from the Castle gateway back round to the top of the town, either back along the path outside the western curtain-wall, or down the Castle drive-way and along the road.   Steps go down beside the Sun Inn. (If you are unable to tackle steps use the road). Descend to the riverside and walk along The Butts.

To those expecting the archery grounds of olde England, the Butts may be a disappointment: the name almost certainly refers to the short butte-ends of land left over from the burgages along the riverbank.

But whatever else, this is a place of beauty, with the quiet deep river and the wooded cliffs opposite. Sit on the seat and drink it in.

● The <u>presbyterian church</u> (now United Reformed) dates from 1828.

● The <u>schools</u> are built on the "lord's waste" beside the river. First, near the bridge, the Borough school-house was built by a beneficiary for the town in 1736. This became the school-master's house for the National School, built alongside in 1824.

● The Coquet below Warkworth is an excellent place to see herons, standing quietly in the far shallows stalking their prey, or flapping lazily overhead. But for nearly 4 years, from spring 1973 until Christmas Eve 1976 it was the home for an unusual visitor: <u>Percy the Pelican</u> became a familiar sight on the river or the cricket field. Now his stuffed remains may be seen in the Hancock Museum in Newcastle.

<u>Bridge End House</u> stands next to the Norman gatehouse. Built in the early eighteenth century, it is easily the most magnificent house in the town. It has managed to retain its iron railings and gate, so many of which went for scrap as a public morale booster during the Second War.

<u>The burgages</u> are the long narrow strips of land that stretch all the way from the houses of the town down to the river (apart from the butt-ends already met).

This is the mediaeval pattern that has survived until today with remarkably little change, even though the houses in the town have been rebuilt. The best overview of them is from the castle keep, but the path from bridge to castle, a right-of-way for hundreds of years, cuts right across them, cutting the gardens in two.

Despite their great length many are kept in immaculate condition – there must be some keen gardeners in Warkworth!

* Beside the small public garden opposite the bridge gatehouse a path disappears between trees and high walls towards the top of the town. Follow this path between the walls, hedges and fences, enjoying the garden scenes, until you debouch onto the road before the Sun Inn.

Here, at the top of the town, you can decide whether the trip to the Hermitage — or another of the walks out of town — is just the thing to complete your day, or would be better if deferred to a fresh day.

The Sun Hotel

Warkworth 20: Walk to the Hermitage

Before you set off, do note that the Hermitage is on the far bank of the river, and can only be visited if the English Heritage warden is on duty with his ferry. The Castle folk will tell you the opening days and times. There is a fee for visits to the Hermitage (ferry included!)

Even if the ferry is inoperative, the walk up the river to the landing is charming, at any time of year, with trees, wildlife and woodland flowers as well as the Coquet.

* From the castle gateway follow the path round the west curtain wall almost to the town. Just by the west postern turn sharply back down a path to the riverside.

Pass the hire-boat landing, and walk upstream. You will pass Queen Alexandra's Landing, and, round the bend, the concrete outlet for the waterworks above Coquet Lodge. Go on past a stile and join the tarmac track that comes down from Howlet Hall for a few metres until you reach the ferry landing. (All that is visible on the far bank is the hut and landing — the Hermitage is totally hidden by centuries-old yew trees.

2.0 kilometres ⎫ Castle to Hermitage
1¼ miles ⎭ and back to town.

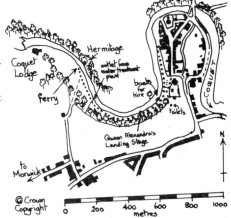

• Boats may be hired (in season) for you to row upstream (or down). Note, however, that you are not allowed to land on the Hermitage bank from hire boats.

• Queen Alexandra's landing stage was built especially for her visit. For some years the Hermitage ferry ran from here.

*Return to Warkworth by the same route

Warkworth 22 : The Hermitage.

The Hermitage is in the care of English Heritage, and may only be visited when the custodian / ferryman is present. There is an entrance fee, and an excellent detailed guide-book.

Reading the guidebooks and histories of the Hermitage can not convey the sense of sheer romance that actually being there brings. From the opposite riverbank there is no hint of the site. It is completely hidden behind massive yews, probably as old as the Hermitage itself. But having crossed the river in the ferry — a romantic enough entrance in itself on a good day— you walk along the north bank, past a spring, to enter under the yews into a twilight world.

Up a sweeping stone staircase the chapel doorway is an opening straight into the side of the cliff, flanked by windows of very different sizes. Down below, between cliff and river, the dwelling-house lies a ruin in stone.

- **The chapel and sacristy** are hewn into the sandstone of the cliff. But this is no rough cave. The masons who built this place created a place of beauty: the chapel has three bays, each with the ceiling carved out to represent vaulting, — although this work was never completed. A doorway just opposite the porch leads through into an inner chamber, the sacristy.

The chapel has several features carved from the rock:
- an altar at the east end, incised with 19th century graffiti;
- an ornate window through into the sacristy, near the altar;
- a south-facing window with remains of carved figures in the recess, possibly a Nativity scene;
- another external window, carved in quatrefoil ✧ shape;
- a doorway into the sacristy, above which is a carved shield which bore the instruments of the Passion: spear, sponge, crown of thorns, nails and the Cross, plus an inscription.
- loopholes in the west wall, once allowing the chapel to be viewed from the solar of the house.

- **The living rooms**, below the cliff, comprise kitchen, hall and solar. Little remains of the kitchen, at the foot of the stairs, except the circular base of an oven. A stair-way, now inaccessible, goes up through a cleft in the rock to reach the site of the hermit's garden.

The hall, which boasts a fine fireplace, has the depth of various floods clearly cut into the stone — living here would have its drawbacks!

The solar was above the hall, and included a chamber cut into the cliff at the west end of the chapel.

<u>History</u>. The origins of the chapel are not precisely known.
The site may well have been an ancient site of worship, like
the cup-and-ring marked cliff by the old ford at Morwick,
3km upriver. Here the fresh spring in the cliffs would have been
of importance. It is presumed that one of the Lords Percy
of Warkworth had the chapel built in the fourteenth century.
The Scottish assault on the town in 1341 might explain the
interruption of the carving on the chapel vaulting. The Percy
family maintained a chaplain here, with a fairly decent living—
this was not a retreat into poverty. But by 1567 the family
had other interests and the hermitage was mentioned in the
estate surveys in the past tense.
There are, of course, various legends of its origin, tales of love
and passion, death and remorse — but you would expect that here!

● <u>Warkworth Harbour</u>. Until 1765 the Coquet performed a last loop before entering the sea more or less opposite the road from Warkworth, through the dunes. Beacon Hill used to be on the south side of the river – it still marks the boundary of Amble (As it is now inconveniently sited from Amble's point of view, Beacon Hill was ignored for the Armada 400 celebrations, in favour of a brazier erected next to the new marina). In 1765 the river changed course, and the old harbour silted up. Part of it is sealed in behind Castle's Dike (named after the constructor, not Warkworth Castle). At low tide much of the old harbour is mud-flats, with attendant bird-life.

● <u>Amble Harbour</u>. After its change of course the Coquet reached the sea by a variety of routes through the dunes, leaving a series of islands and an unnavigable sand-bar. From 1836 the problem was solved by building the break-waters to channel the river flow. Staithes to handle the coal traffic from Broomhill colliery followed, and the town developed. Now Amble is recovering from the coal traffic, and developing as a resort.

The north breakwater was extensively rebuilt and reinforced during the 1980's, occasioning the temporary road beside Warkworth Harbour, for construction traffic.

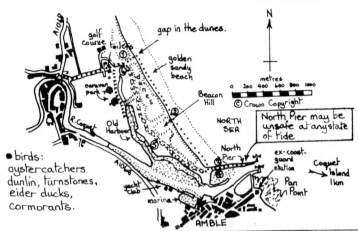

golf course toilets

gap in the dunes.

golden sandy beach

caravan park

Old Harbour

R. Coquet

Beacon Hill

NORTH SEA

North Pier

NORTH

ex-coast-guard station

North Pier may be unsafe at any state of tide

Coquet Island 1 km

Pan Point

yacht club

marina

AMBLE

metres
0 200 400 600 800 1000
© Crown Copyright.

• birds:
oyster-catchers
dunlin, turnstones,
eider ducks,
cormorants.

✱ Cross the Norman bridge and follow the 'Cemetery' sign-post,
up the tree-lined side-road to the east. Continue to a cross-
roads. (To the south is a caravan park, to the north a golf course).
Go straight on, down the path between the car-parks. Pass
over the flat area (the old harbour/river mouth) and reach
the beach, through a gap in the dunes.
Turn south along the strand of fine sand towards the river-
mouth, until you reach the breakwater. Note the warning signs.
The track beside the old harbour is not a right of way, but
provides a convenient return route. It may be flooded – beware!
Note how the high watch-tower of the castle is visible for most
of this return walk to the town.

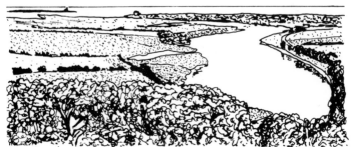

View from the Castle down-river towards Amble and Coquet Island.

---

* Follow the A1068 road out of Warkworth, past the Castle and down to the riverside. (The footpath along from the Butts, shown on O.S. maps, may exist legally, but not in practice). A decent footpath, separated from the road by a wide verge, takes you alongside the river, downstream past the semi-tidal weir. Continue until you reach a gateway opening on to the Braid.....

Warkworth Castle from the east

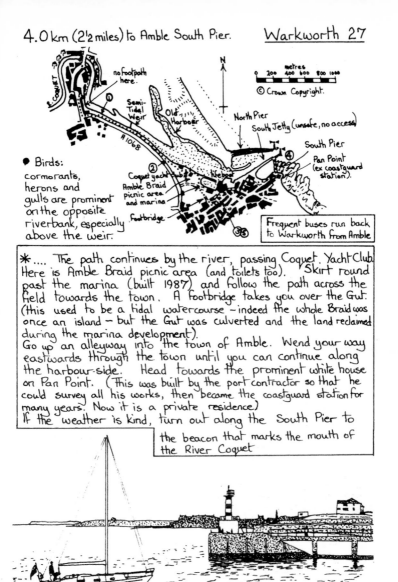

Birds:
cormorants,
herons and
gulls are prominent
on the opposite
riverbank, especially
above the weir.

Frequent buses run back
to Warkworth from Amble

* .... The path continues by the river, passing Coquet Yacht Club.
Here is Amble Braid picnic area (and toilets too).   Skirt round
past the marina (built 1987) and follow the path across the
field towards the town.   A footbridge takes you over the Gut.
(This used to be a tidal watercourse – indeed the whole Braid was
once an island – but the Gut was culverted and the land reclaimed
during the marina development).
Go up an alleyway into the town of Amble. Wend your way
eastwards through the town until you can continue along
the harbour-side.   Head towards the prominent white house
on Pan Point. (This was built by the port contractor so that he
could survey all his works, then became the coastguard station for
many years. Now it is a private residence)
If the weather is kind, turn out along the South Pier to
the beacon that marks the mouth of
the River Coquet

Warkworth Index

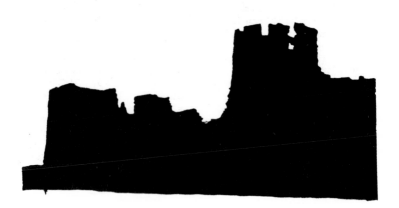

Bibliography:

The following books have been informative:

County History of Northumberland.		1899	(N.C.C)
Northumberland,	N. Pevsner	1957	(Penguin)
Northumbria.	E. Grierson	1976	(Collins)
Northumbrian Heritage.	N. Ridley	1965	(R. Hale)
Portrait of Northumberland,	N. Ridley	1965	(R. Hale)
Highways and Byways in N'land,	P. Anderson Graham	1920	(Macmillan)
The Queen's England, N'land.	A. Mee et al	1952	(N. Ed. Ctee)
Companions into N'land.	S. Moorhouse	1953	(Methuen)
Discovering Northumberland.	T.H. Rowland	1973	(F. Graham)
Mediaeval Castles, Towers, etc.	T.H. Rowland	1987	(TH Rowland)
Parish Church of St. Lawrence, Warkworth.			
Warkworth Castle		1988	(Eng. Her.)
Warkworth Hermitage		1985	(H&MCE.)
Bothal Observed	R. Bibby	1973	(F. Graham)
Bygone Morpeth	T.H. Rowland	1989	(Phillimore)
Town Trails for Morpethians	A. H. Tweddle		
Curiosities of N'land	Armstrong et al	1970	(F. Graham)
Alnwick	F. Graham		(Butler + Butler)
District of Alnwick Visitors' Guide			(Home.)
Alnwick Castle	English Life	1980	
Rural Branch Lines of N'land.	C.R. Warn	1975	(F. Graham)
Border Country Branch Lines	N. Caplan	1981	(Ian Allan)
N.E. Branch Lines since 1925	K. Hoole	1978	(Ian Allan)
Green Tracks & Heather Tracks	Wade, Balmain		(H.O. Wade)
Looking Around N'land.	Harry Rowland	1979	(H. Rowland)
The Reivers' Way	H.O. Wade	1977	(F. Graham)
Cragside – the Power Circuit.		1988	(Nat. Trust)
Heart of Northumberland	J. Salwey	1949	(St. Catherine)
Woodland Walks in N. England.	G. Wilkinson	1986	(Webb + Bower)
Castles and Houses in Britain,	Country Life	1986	(Newnes)
The Border Reivers	G. Watson	1974	(R. Hale)
Northumberland Nat. Park.	T. Hopkins	1987	(Webb+Bower)
Northumberland Nat. Park.	J. Philipson	1969	(HMSO)
Northumberland Villages	G. Watson	1976	(R. Hale)
Walks in Coquetdale	N'land. C.C.	1986	(N.C.C.)

Answer: National Rivers Authority hydrometrics station, for measuring river flow. The instruments can be dangled from the pulley for the operator to position, so that the amount of water in the river flow can be calculated.

● The Book House,
half-way up Castle Street
in Warkworth is the home
of Sandhill Press. Here
also is a homely bookshop.
Drop in and buy something,
preferably another of
the author's books!

Other titles from Sandhill
Press are listed opposite.

● The Author.

Odd as it may seem, Ian Smith is not a native of these
parts. Although he has been in love with Northumberland
—and one of its girls — for over twenty years, he actually
lives in Thornaby, on the Tees. His origins are even
further afield, not even in the North: he hales from
Bromley in Kent! Having destroyed some people's illusions,
he hastily adds that he much prefers the North, and
Northumberland in particular!
Ian is a physics teacher, daily in touch with a high
technology world of equipment and computing. The
walking, photography, drawing and hand-writing is
a nice contrast.

Also by Ian Smith: Northumbrian Coastline
                      Warkworth (separately).
                      Yorkshire Coastline

Also published by Sandhill Press:

Northumbria in Pictures.   Beryl Sanderson.
The Last Years of a Frontier.   D. L. W. Tough.
"As they were" from old photographs.   R. Thompson Dix
The Border Reivers.   Godfrey Watson.
Upper Coquetdale, Northumberland.   David Dippie Dixon.
Victorian and Edwardian Northumbria.   J.W. Thompson & D. Bond.
The Northumbrian Pub: an architectural history.
                                        Lynn F. Pearson.
Ghosts and legends of Northumbria   Sandhill Press.
The Body in the Bank: famous Northern murders.
                                        Sandhill Press.
Rogues and Reivers of the North Country Sandhill Press.
A Basinful o' Geordie   Dorfy
Mad Dogs & Cyclists : on two wheels in Northumbria
                                        Chris Rooney.

Mediæval Castles, Towers, Peles and Bastles of N'land
                                        T. H. Rowland.
The Great Gunmaker: a life of Lord Armstrong. David Dougan.
Customs and Traditions of Northumbria. Sandhill Press.
Myth and Magic of Northumbria.   Sandhill Press.

sandhill press

17 Castle Street, Warkworth
MORPETH, Northumberland.
NE65 0UW